SET UP AS A

MICRO PUBLISHER

Avoid the Pitfalls and Publish for Profit

Jennifer Lancaster

Power of Words

ISBN 978-1-7640633-0-2 (pbk)

Author: www.jenniferlancaster.com.au/books
Email: enquiry@jenniferlancaster.com.au

Give feedback on the book at:
Amazon, Goodreads.

NATIONAL LIBRARY OF AUSTRALIA

A catalogue record for this book is available from the National Library of Australia

Motto: Be Prepared

"Another way to be prepared is to think negatively. Yes, I'm a great optimist. but, when trying to make a decision, I often think of the worst case scenario. I call it 'the eaten by wolves factor.'

If I do something, what's the most terrible thing that could happen? Would I be eaten by wolves? One thing that makes it possible to be an optimist is if you have a contingency plan for when all hell breaks loose. There are a lot of things I don't worry about, because I have a plan in place if they do."

Randy Pausch, The Last Lecture

Contents

The Preface...   1
    Why read this book?   1
    Are you ready for the truth?   2

1. Publishing Myths and Assumptions, Busted!   5
    What are your chances, income wise?   7

2. A Business Mindset Shift   9
    Many Obstacles   10
    What Flavour is Book Sales Success?   11

3. Publishing Business Model Choices   13
    1. Traditional Publishing   13
    2. Self-Publishing   14
    3. Hybrid or Vanity Publishing   16
    4. Micro Publishing   17
    5. Print on Demand (POD)   18
    6. Crowdfunding   19
    7. Collaborative Publishing   19

4. Tips for Independent Publishing in Australia   21
    Fearlessly Buy Your ISBNs   22
    Understand Basic Copyright Law and Defamation Law   23

5. Micro Publishing in Depth   25
    Structure of the Publishing House   25
    Company, Partnership or Trust?   25
    Insurance   26
    Bookkeeping   26
    Beg, Hire or Learn These Production Skills   27
    The Low vs High Content Debate   28

6. Suggested Budget Breakdown   31
    Amazon Marketing Strategy   35
    Ghostwriters and Editors?   38
    Make a Valid Publishing Contract   39

7. Markets, Not Marketplaces   43
    It's Demand and Supply, Damn Fool!   43
    Market Strategy   44
    What Influences Book Buying?   47
    Ins and Outs of Audiobooks   49

8. Marketing   51
    Go-To-Market Plan   52
    Pleasing Your Market   55

9. Marketing Secrets and Optimisation   61
    Publisher Website   61
    1: Check out all Book Listings across all Retailer Sites   63
    2: Get Reviews via Niche Bloggers   63
    3: Write Articles with Sales Page Links   64
    4: Run a Reader Giveaway   65
    5. Build a Community First   66
    6. Analyse Categories but don't Paralyse   68
    7. Paid Shortcut: Launch Tools   68
    8. Advertising and Promotion: KDP   69
    9. Make Friends with Meta   73

10. The 'Cheap eBook' Strategy   75
    About Kindle Select and their Deals and Promotions   75
    Australian-Based Book Promotions   77

11. The 'Viral Message' Book Strategy   81
    Book Positioning   81
    Attracting Clients   82
    Sell More with a Great Blurb   83

12. Sales Funnels - the Hidden Secrets of the Online Gurus   87

Why are Author Newsletters a Dream Tactic?   88

'Free to Buy, Pay to Ship' Sales Funnel   89

13. Publishing Tools - for Micros & Author Agents   91
    Ways to Sell Books Directly   94

14. Publishing Tools for Self-Published Authors   99
    Reedsy Studio   99
    Vellum vs Atticus   100
    eBook Conversion Types   101
    Asana – an App to Manage Launches   101
    Audiobooks with ACX Tools   102
    Google Play Books – free Narration   102
    PayHip   102
    New IngramSpark Decisions   103
    Making Smart Royalty Decisions – IngramSpark   104
    For Those Going through KDP Print   107
    Pleasing Retailers & Suppliers   107

15. Reviews   111

16. Writing Hacks to Save Time   113
    Research Before You Write   113
    Organising Your Topics with Mind Mapping   114
    Sharpening the Saw   115
    Identifying Themes in Your Writing   116
    Turning Your Blog into a Book   116
    Editing the Book   119
    Final Steps in Preparing Your Book   120
    Distribution Options   123

Little Black Book   127

Jennifer Lancaster

The Preface...

Why read this book?

Save yourself the school of hard knocks. After 12 years of book marketing and hearing the woes of other authors, I continually look for solutions to the problem of lower-than-desired sales. Is it an app, a platform I'm missing, a press opportunity I need or people just don't like my titles? Ouch!

Rather than paying for everything, an 'indie' is someone who learns the parts they can. Micro Publishers are indies evolving; they might offer a niche themselves, write and publish a fiction book series, or publish other people's books on a theme. My definition is quite diverse and it's more about taking a professional approach.

Okay, but why should an Indie become a Micro Publisher?

Firstly, everything will look more professional with publication branding. With smoother processes, you won't go mad... so that's another benefit. In this book, you will also learn how to think about markets and selling in a new way. Fresh thinking is urgently required in this industry, as one of the most competitive industries around!

This book helps you to get to know the world of a niche micro publisher and the tactics of this cluey set... before you start and find out later that you bought the ticket but the ride was CRAZY.

Are you ready for the truth?

If you've dipped a toe into book writing and publishing, you may be wondering why it's not been a massive success… why you can't find a book selling angle that works.

It's not just you who's thinking this. We are all snowed into thinking that it's easy to create a publishing business on the side of a job or spin that plate while coaching others. This 'easy street' notion is ridiculously untrue. Publishers must be hyper-efficient in all they do.

Being efficient is a great idea, but it's not only productivity that will help you. Whether it's the 10X, more driven approach or the stress-free productivity style you take, to be successful you also need to have the resilient determination of a mule.

Good news… If you have the right mindset for dedication and focus (and, let's face it, a first world education), your chances for success go skywards. 'Consuming a lot of information' is how Peter Holmquist started out. He is a small publisher who is in the top .002% of Amazon KDP earners. He has a system, a team to do some of the work, and 1,552 books on sale. (Peter's tips are featured later in this book, although this level is higher than we're aiming for).

Unfortunately, with aging parents, potentially children, other career work and our health to juggle, most 35 to 60 year-old women are not able to simply emulate this type of prolific publishing. For this subset of potential micro publishers, a scaled down version is proposed—though still with an eye for profit.

There are many myths and assumptions about publishing I'll uncover in this book. A lot of these myths are being fed by businesspeople who advertise about wonderful results in order to sell their expensive courses. Some are assumptions which are due to a misunderstanding of 'marketplace' versus 'market attraction' as a sales process. This will all be explained so that you can spend more time on market attraction and less time on worrying about the dwindling KDP payouts.

Another problem is that novices in publishing don't have the many and varied skills that can make this book publishing thing profitable, so they rely heavily on others. They either hire these skills directly, from freelance designers, editors and marketing consultants, or they buy a hybrid/subsidy publishing package and lose all control over the process while getting little results from doing so. I don't want this for you!

Choose your niche and deeply know your market. You need to understand the world you're trying to achieve in. Writers attend writing workshops, but what you need more of is marketing and strategic business education. Publishing has a lot more to it than the technical details – so let's learn now!

———————————

1

Publishing Myths and Assumptions, Busted!

Publishing on Amazon has become the promised gold mine of our time… or is it fool's gold? The number of Facebook groups talking about 'KDP' or self-publishing have exploded, gurus teaching easy self-publishing have popped up like Wack-a-mole, and the number of 'publishing' companies who charge still proliferate. (There are 70 publishers listed as accepting unsolicited books in the APA directory yet only a dozen of these don't charge).

Self-publishing books on your favourite topics is seen as untapped gold, whereas (when considering the billions in revenue from e-learning) most money in the industry is being made by people selling the shovels (production services) and online courses to dig the gold.

Consider this stat: 28,234 titles were published in Australia in 2023. Meanwhile, a lot of bestselling books selling well here originate from the US or UK. A large Australian distributor, United Book Distributors, had stock of 63,000 titles in the warehouse in 2023. This is enormous!

On the bright side, a Rise Bookselling report said that 64% of Australians bought a book in 2023. Do you reckon that of those in the 64% of 21 million adults, you could identify a particular niche readership? (Also remembering that the largest proportion of the purchases are for popular fiction or the odd memoir by Prince Harry).

The 2024 bust-up of a subsidy publisher, Shawline Publishing, put the realities of independent publishing into perspective. The authors were suspicious if they got the right royalties or not, which is fair considering they didn't get much for their money, not even a final manuscript file. The collapse of saw around 70 authors left without completed services and $5,500 to $7,000 out of pocket. I've heard these stories for years, with the most recent being Ocean Reeve Publishing, who went into liquidation with no notice.

Another problem is 'sharks' find this industry an easy play. They can ask $5K for a book to be produced and somewhat edited and get willing participants. And if the publishing financials are unsound, this type of thing happens:

'We paid Ocean in full for 1000 books in March 2024. It is now October and the books are nowhere to be seen and he has stopped communicating and gone underground. We have now referred the matter to a Solicitor for a Statutory Demand.' (Facebook review)

In other cases, could it be that the book didn't earn them? Publishing is an expensive sport and creating real title winners is not easy. Adding to the barriers, authors paying for the editing and production doesn't mean that the book is saleable or the marketing will be done adequately. Promotion often falls on the shoulders of those who know the least about marketing: the author.

When normally critical authors get promises that their book will soon be in theirs and others' hands, their judgement is impaired. Even when doing due diligence, there are too many sad stories, too many poor services, and people who have been let down.

Be scam aware for all things literary, including fake literary agents, scam publishers, etc at Writer Beware (*https://writerbeware.blog/scam-archive/*). Be aware that if the publisher is based in Australia you can seek reparation through the Office of Fair Trading and small claims. If the publisher is based overseas from you, you cannot do much after the initial complaint. However, never pay to get back 'rights' to a book that went nowhere amid the production. These scammers rarely sue because guess what? They wouldn't win.

What are your chances, income wise?

Four hundred years after the invention of the Gutenberg Press, give or take, novice authors are still expecting books once 'in print' to be like a flame-thrower of money towards their account. Like other industries though, a few well-known people sell a disproportionate number of books. Consider those with huge audiences, e.g., Mel Robbins, Brendon Burchard, and in Australia, David Koch and Victoria Devine. They sell big, because they have a reputation for quality.

The reality of absolute novices making a full-time wage from print on demand or Kindle publishing is ludicrous. There are videos claiming 'a single Mum with no writing skills made $4,000 a month from KDP'. Okay, if this is true, what did she spend on ghostwriting, book design and advertising? Be aware that there are costs involved in publishing and that $4,000 claimed could be solely the launch month of a book, with declining numbers afterward. It would require quite a lot of promos and Amazon Ads to achieve.

Most micro publishers don't get a hit book the first time, just as traditional publishers don't, but you could pour your efforts into researching a niche and experimenting so that on your third, fourth or fifth book, chances are high to get the income returns and lifestyle you seek.

Author-First Results. In a research survey on self-publishing author income, ALLi has released *the Big Indie Author Data Drop*. The median incomes found were US: $5,000 (Author's Guild, USD), Canada: C9,380, Australia: AU$18,200 ('22), and the ALLi worldwide survey median of $12,749 ('23). The Alliance of Independent Authors made a global survey of over 2000 self-published authors to get an accurate comparison, those who spent over 50% of their working time on writing and publishing.

The Written Word Media Survey (2,000 authors) found that authors doing well use professional cover designers and editors and write prolificly. In December 2023, their survey showed that the median number of books produced was 8 ('median' removes outliers like those with 300+ books). It also showed median time as 15 hours per week spent writing, so these are people who don't outsource that part. BookFunnel was the most used tool for direct sales (40%), followed by Shopify, Woocommerce, and Payhip.[1]

The mean (average income) shown was a lot higher, at US$82,600, because there are a small number of indie authors really thriving (21%) and making between $50,000 and $250,000 per year. In fact, self-published authors make up over 50% of Kindle's Top 400 Books for 2023, say K-lytics. Times have really changed.

Another stat of interest from the WWM survey: of those authors earning $25,000+ per month, income came from an average of 61 titles per author.[2]

✋ Action Jackson:

The way to achieve your income goals is to set and write down realistic goals. Acknowledge the need for outside skills in your goals, and the fact that most small book publishers are spending 20 to 30% on marketing. Will you consider this as a business?

Some say that a systematic process is even better, to take you towards that goal. So, the next step is to put your business goal into action and create a marketing and sales plan.

2

A Business Mindset Shift

'The only way to make your present better is to make your future bigger' - Dan Sullivan

Linear, reachable goals are what most of us aim for. That's why most authors see Amazon KDP (a royalty income pathway) as a perfect goal for them. They don't even consider the long road of building up an author name website, running a creative vlog or podcast, and spreading their message via all media (mass media and social). It all seems too hard. Plus, being on video or interviews brings up the dreaded imposter syndrome. The goal of publishing books on KDP and the milestone of posting covers on Facebook are reachable – but deficient.

'10X is Easier Than 2X', written by Dr. Benjamin Hardy with ideas from Dan Sullivan, explores the power of adopting a 10x mindset. A 10x mindset requires letting go of 80% of your current ways, embracing new approaches, and even adopting a new identity. In contrast, a 2x mindset involves only a 20% change, which is often how those on the growth path envision their next level of growth. Interestingly, despite Dr. Hardy's significant contribution to the book, he did not receive an equal share of the book's revenues, highlighting that sometimes key learnings extend beyond the content itself. Always check the rights on the publisher's contract.

Riding along with the myth that putting out Kindle books is 'the key to riches' is the belief that the world is moving against you as a creator. Yet, is there any point in saying 'AI-generated content is taking over, I can't win'. Or is it more fruitful to ask, 'Why do people always buzz straight to fresh and value-rich ideas?' And, 'what concepts and solutions will be extra meaningful in this new world?'

Because you don't get anywhere with tiny steps and copycat plays, let's aim for the goals which aren't just a beginner's folly.

✋ Actioning Goals

Figure out what kind of things you should watch to influence your new publishing path. Should you watch marketing forecasts and long psychology (TEDX) talks on video rather than watching moon-walking blokes on reels?

Should you become part of a supportive and relevant community (e.g. in Skool, there are many) rather than join a moaning novice self-published author Facebook group? Think of the best path where your personal growth and professional learning are uplifted. In-person business networking groups are also a great way to collaborate with like minds. Look for ones that meet regularly and only charge for appetizers, not memberships.

(This Skool is a platform where leaders run their 'community', including courses. Many are free to attend; some are paid memberships.)

Many Obstacles

There are so many obstacles to publishing for profit, but a big one is gossip and social media distractions. It's time to focus only on the pinnacle of useful actions and let the rest go. You must decide on the most productive and relevant course of action (including branding and marketing) based on your large goal, while letting go of all the little time-consuming things that others might consider needed. After all, small tactics can overshadow a bigger strategy of inspiring others to join your mission. Some let go of trying to go viral on Instagram after fruitless hours. Some let go of finding that elusive expert on marketing and execute one thing well themselves, e.g. podcasting. Others let go of hoping for useful opinions on their new books from family or reviews from friends who don't even read books.

Publishing is about running a tight ship and it's not the time for reactionary thinking.

> 'Chance favors the prepared. Prepared in publishing = good books, good covers, good blurb, good web site, good backlist, good craft, consistent releases, and a grasp of basic marketing skills. The only part we have control over? Prepared. So that is what we should do. Then we're ready if luck lightning strikes.' – DG, Kindle writer

Taking the next three months as a sprint, what three goals are you aiming for?

What Flavour is Book Sales Success?

Now, there is success. Denise Duffield-Thomas has a niche audience in Australia who love her work. She writes and speaks on creating wealth abundance. It's an attractive topic. She tells others wanting to write to 'set an intention for your dream book'. Duffield-Thomas was self-published, successful with her money bootcamps and blog, when a commissioning editor from Hay House asked to pitch her book ideas to her boss. Well, that just doesn't happen to people without a large list and audience, as I've come to learn from unsuccessful novice authors. (https://www.denisedt.com/writing-a-book-is-smart).

She got her idea for 'Lucky Bitch' in the shower after asking the universe. Get Rich, Lucky Bitch followed, then Chillpreneur, advice for female business owners. If you've got a degree or otherwise research-centric, you're probably rolling your eyes right now at the titles. But this stuff sells.

Do you know what else sells? Promises. Promises of wealth, abundance, great abs, thin thighs and how to attract others. Not just that; there are a lot of best-sellers in business. Look at Russell Brunson, who wrote the Underground Secrets series for Dotcom, Web traffic and funnels. He certainly did very well.

It was almost as if he planned to have bestselling books that educated people on the need for funnels and then sell them an expensive software that sets up sales funnels… oh, wait.

Here are some who have jumped on the bandwagon of side hustle + six figures. Note the similarity of goal but diversity of markets.

- *Six Figure Author: Using Data to Sell Books* - Chris Fox (who writes on side hustles)
- *Six Figures in School Hours* - Kate Toon (who is a digital entrepreneur and Mum)
- *Six Figure Sales Recruiter* - Ryan Hohman
- *Secrets of the Six Figure Yoga Teacher* - Cate Stillman and Kevin Rineer

All this is telling me that it's time to think of a different idea and a new tune to whistle, even though wealth is that eternal promise.

Simplifying wildly, there are four promises to choose from: better health, better relationships, more wealth, and self-control.

Do you want to make waves? Then craft a new looking speedboat. We do that through the clever use of language. When using 'hook' language, you need to be careful that you're giving a message that large swathes of the buying public understand and relate to. More on this in 'The Viral Message Book Strategy' later in the book.

3

Publishing Business Model Choices

1. Traditional Publishing

Seen as 'the way it was' prior to 2005, traditional publishing involves authors submitting original manuscripts to established publishing houses. If accepted, the publisher handles editing, design, distribution, and marketing. The real benefit here is the distribution channel to bricks and mortar bookstores. However, that anticipated benefit dwindles as real bookstores go out of business.

The cited averages of between 90% to 95% rejection rates by major publishers certainly don't make it easy for authors. With relevance to their imprint and the sheer number of submissions the stated reason for this, there is a further harsh truth: audience is everything. Those who already have an audience (a comedian, a known artist, a loved influencer) are sought after – if their manuscript makes sense to the acquiring editor. A penchant for publicity is ideal.

A small window of hope for alumni of any tertiary institution: University presses typically have a slightly lower rejection rate compared to major commercial publishers, often around 70% to 90%. They tend to publish fewer titles than major publishers, focusing on quality and academic merit.

Considerations: While this model offers authors street credibility and resources, it is competitive and time-consuming. Authors typically receive 10% royalties but may not earn any if getting a large advance. Traditional publishing, with its gatekeepers and long submission process in many cases, suits only those who can brush off rejection.

Sales is not a given: a trial of five large publishers in the US noted, '90% of traditionally published books sell fewer than 2000 units – and half sell fewer than a dozen books' (shared by Dean Wesly Smith).

BookPeople put out a seasonal 'Reading Guide' and this guide helps independent booksellers market and sell hot books, knowing what is going on. They also give posters and shelf-talkers. The top 10 bestsellers shown on the Book-People website are all traditionally published. Not an accident.

Traditional authors, watch out for returns and other hidden costs, including distribution. Say you have found a well-reputed publisher (e.g. Fontaine). Each larger publisher works with a book distributor (in addition to a wholesaler like Ingram Book Company), which generally charges a 25% distribution fee on customer sales, plus a 10% re-stocking fee on returns. An example of a book distributor is Penguin Random House Distribution, based in Victoria, who are huge.

Writer Beware says: 'Working with a distributor is an advantage, as it raises the likelihood of the publisher's books making it into brick-and-mortar stores, which in turn may result in better sales – but it also lowers royalties, since those fees, deducted by the distributor, reduce sales income to the publisher and thus the amount on which your royalties are calculated.' This is why many authors, who are creative, talented and known, are generally underwhelmed with their royalties.

2. Self-Publishing

The first self-publisher and artist known was William Blake (1757-1827). He was deeply invested in integrating imagery and text, considering the entirety to be of equal importance, and he and his wife hand illustrated and bound each book. [3]

The excitement of self-publishing spread throughout the world starting in about 2006, and while numbers of titles launching are still humongous, reality is setting in. Competition isn't just fierce, it's ridiculous. Each year, an estimated 1.4 million new titles are published annually through KDP alone. Amazon's market share in the US is 80% of all books.[4]

In this model, authors take full control of the publishing process, from writing to marketing. This can be done through platforms like Amazon Kindle Direct Publishing (KDP), Blurb or IngramSpark.

Considerations: Higher profit margins (up to 70% royalties), but authors must manage all aspects, including costs for editing, cover design, and marketing. Marketing is usually where it all falls apart.

'Modern writers must make the mental shift to embrace the sponsorship model. It doesn't have to be your only source of income, but it should be on your radar. For most of us, our work is never going to appear on the shelves of brick and mortar bookstores. I've come to accept that this is an advantage.'
– Walter Rhein, Substack.

Platforms

If you don't want to hire freelancers or learn, there are places that help bring the services together. The following are services done for you, though to what quality I'm not sure. Perhaps not something to order if building a book publishing brand – unless you believe true independent publishing is technically too challenging.

BookBaby - find editing, formatting, ebook conversion, cover design services, order print proofs, get books distributed and access basic marketing tools. You can order editing stand alone or as a package but maybe forgo distribution, as adding global distribution costs US$399.

Although BookBaby state they offer high-quality physical copies, generally, the print prices are a little more than I'd pay with IngramSpark.

Spines - this newer platform leverages AI technology to provide services for all book formats, including Print-on-Demand (POD), eBooks, and audiobooks. The dashboard facilitates every step, from proofreading and editing to formatting and cover design. Spines also ensures global distribution. They plan to spit out 8,000 books per year, attracting criticism from some writers, who express concerns about the potential impact on quality and creative processes. While Spines may talk about 100 channels all they like, ensure that humans are involved in your book editing process. Package pricing is from US$1,478 on up + $200 'membership' including Kindle upload and royalty management. 100% royalties to authors. While it's easier for those older self-publishers, it seems way too expensive for multi-publishers.

Tablo offered 'socially shared publishing' and the automation mangled a book I made there, royalties were non-existent, and it seems this kind of platform-based publishing sites aren't very good.

3. Hybrid or Vanity Publishing

Also called Subsidy, this is a blend of traditional and self-publishing. Authors pay for some services (like editing and design) while retaining more control and a higher percentage of royalties. There are few hybrid publishers who are legitimately offering you something more than production done.

This model, however, could be beneficial for authors who want professional support but don't want to learn all about book design and publishing. Look for reputable hybrid publishers in Australia, with leaders who think in high quality terms. If you want delivery of your designed digital files, always ask up-front. Self-Publishing Australia offers a commercial package that includes these.

Generally, US-based companies such as Balboa Press, Xlibris, Trafford, Austin Macauley, et al do not supply any designed files. These are considered vanity presses. Regarding publishing with Xlibris, a paying author told me he would be charged AU $15 per book to order his own books, after paying between $1,999 and $5,000 for a package. (He requested his formatted PDF so he could get a local printer to print it. Smart.) Customers pay $499 to set their own price, rather than the inflated book price Author Solutions Inc will set for any book. This is unconscionable. You can read some publisher reviews at ProductReviews.com.au or at TrustPilot.com.

These vanity publishers don't care about results. Before you go to pay to publish, check the company out at *https://writerbeware.blog*.

Let's look at a positive case of publishing. Therese Tarlinton hybrid-published *'SWAP: Marketing Without Money'* (2022, KMD Books). For her book, she has received 14 5-star Amazon reviews and won an ABLE Award. KMD Books (Karen McDermott) do Thought Leader/celebrity publishing and quality seems high, although there is no way they could afford to be in business without charging something up front. Judging by their Facebook page, KMD does 'cover reveals' and publicity, and they have a modern website bookstore. They use Peribo Distribution to bookstores: something of an anomaly among subsidy publishers.

If you're setting up a publishing brand, ensure you build a solid reputation, process and online assets as these better hybrids.

4. Micro Publishing

These are small-scale publishing operations that often focus on niche markets or specific genres. Micro publishers publish a small number of titles per year, but usually more than three. As there are lots of advantages of this model, we'll go deep later.

Considerations: This model allows for more creative freedom and community engagement. Micro publishers often rely on local distribution networks and guerilla marketing strategies.

As an aspiring publisher, high street bookstore distribution is tempting. As I write how-to and other books, I once investigated the cost of placing a large order with a printer, generating publicity and going through a distributor (very few left). After the distributor/retail chunk of 70% of RRP and shipping to factory, there would have been little to no royalty left for me, the creator, and quite a big risk.

To publish successfully, you'll need to understand the market, so research book trends, genres, and reader preferences (see later in the book). The Australian Publishers Association (APA) provides valuable insights and they offer a publishing membership, or you might prefer the analytical path and start to use a book category and keyword analysis tool.

5. Print on Demand (POD)

Many get printing and print on demand (POD) mixed up, but offset printing and POD are two very different book printing methods. With POD, authors can allow for the printing of their books as orders come in, reducing upfront costs and inventory risks.

Services like Lulu and Blurb are popular, as well as localised services like IngramSpark and KDP. Localised means wherever the person lives, as they will print and ship from the closest print facility. Royalties are complex, so will be discussed later in this book.

One expectation is that printing via demand is going to mean easy selling and great profits. This is not true: Bulk print orders still have the best profit per book and promotion is needed in order to find sales.

Considerations: While POD is cost-effective to set up, the per-unit cost is a little higher than 300+ copies offset printing, particularly those printing in China. On the plus side, the risk of unsold books is far less. It's essential to price books accordingly and play around with pricing in the platform's royalty calculator.

6. Crowdfunding

Authors can use platforms like Kickstarter or Pozible to raise funds for their book projects before publication. It can be difficult, nigh on impossible, if you're not used to sharing massively on social media and don't have an email list. Pozible takes 5% of amount raised plus 1.75% transaction fee. A successful pre-sale can possibly put you in front of small presses or literary agents.

Considerations: This model can help gauge interest and build a community around the book. Successful campaigns often offer rewards like signed copies or exclusive content. It's necessary to work out expected profits and include for shipping, as sometimes this could be paid for twice.

Overall, a crowdfunding book campaign is a great way to judge popularity prior to listing it on the public publishing marketplace.

7. Collaborative Publishing

Authors team up with other writers or creatives to share resources and expertise. This can include co-publishing or forming a collective. Remember, you are peers, not client and author.

Considerations: Collaboration can reduce costs and expand reach, but it requires clear legal agreements on roles and revenue sharing. The overheads might be considerable if you need to also create a company with shareholders, although contrary to what most think, you can make a company online without an accountant.

4

Tips for Independent Publishing in Australia

Having looked at the main publishing options today, here's a short overview of the things you'll need to plan for as an indie publisher of any size in Australia. We go more into marketing and optimisation in that chapter.

Understand the Market: Research Australian book trends, genres, and reader preferences. The Australian Publishers Association (APA) provides valuable insights.

Networking: Join local writing associations (State based), attend literary festivals, and connect with other authors and publishers. The Australian Society of Authors (ASA) is a good resource.

ISBN and Copyright: Ensure you obtain an ISBN for your book and understand copyright laws in Australia. (See below).

Distribution: Explore local bookstores and library suppliers. Only consider partnering with a big distributor if you are planning to distribute over five print books per year and don't mind financial risk. If you want national bookstore/ Big W distribution, then you need a book publishing advanced schedule, a team, an APA membership, a marketing plan, and to get in touch with distributors for their other specifications. Lisa Messenger is an Australian who has done this with her company's support, Messenger Publishing.

If you're not in a great financial position, then stick to PublishDrive or IngramSpark – aggregators rather than actual retail store distributors.

Marketing planning:

Set up author profiles + publisher profile on three or four social media channels ahead of publication. Bluesky is a good social channel for authors to connect on. Ensure you get an easy to curate website, and email newsletters to build an audience. Engage with readers through book signings and events.

Booko.com.au is a great place to see all the retail prices of each book in one place, and you can save money on book buying if you are an avid reader. You can use Trove to check if a book is in a nearby library.

Fearlessly Buy Your ISBNs

How many ISBNs?

Ensure you obtain an ISBN from MyIdentifiers (Thorpe-Bowker) for your book (or your country's identification supplier) so it registers in Nielsen Books in Print. Get as many ISBNs as foreseen. Most choose the 10-pack, one for each format and a few extra for clients. In Australia, you must pay an additional fee for first-time publishers of $55.

You will need to make a legal deposit at the National Library and (your) state library once your print book is out.

Later ISBNs

There is a myth circulating that once you choose a free 'ISBN' at Kindle, you will not be able to ever take that book to other platforms. That's not true; you can 'unpublish' the title inside your account, purchase and assign an ISBN through the proper provider, use a book cover template generator (free barcode), and then manage all the details of those formats through Thorpe.

Thorpe-Bowker in Oz is named MyIdentifiers.com.au. Or if in New Zealand/ Canada, go through the National Library. Upload a cover image (JPG) that is correct, well in advance of publication. Set your publication date and set your worldwide rights. Many people get flummoxed over all the book types; you are likely to want 'trade book'. Ensure you don't put Amazon for publisher, that is not correct. You can put print on demand or Lightning Source down for distribution and (optionally) your business name for publisher.

Another benefit is, Google can more easily associate your titles with your name when you are the registered author (even if through an imprint name).

Understand Basic Copyright Law and Defamation Law

Learn something about copyright laws in Australia. Never assume or rely on hearsay. The Australian Copyright Council offers guidance in the form of PDFs on quoting, explaining the 10% rule, etc. There is no need to register for copyright in most countries outside the US, as it is implied with the work's copyright/date/author name line.

Resources:

Australian Publishers Association (APA): *https://www.publishers.asn.au*

Australian Society of Authors (ASA): *https://www.asauthors.org*

Australian Copyright Council: *https://www.copyright.org.au*

National Library: *https://www.library.gov.au/services/ publishers-and-self-publishers/international-standard-book-number-isbn*

5

Micro Publishing in Depth

Structure of the Publishing House

Congratulations! You've got an idea for a micro publishing house and a cool name. Now it's time to get a professional perspective. Is that name registerable at ASIC? Can you get the domain name? Do these searches:

Availability of Business name:
https://connectonline.asic.gov.au/RegistrySearch/

Trademark (e.g. for product names, to avoid competition and take-down orders): *https://ipaustralia.gov.au/trade-marks/*

Domain Name Search: *https://webcentral.au/domains*

Company, Partnership or Trust?

If already a businessperson, then take an accountant's advice on whether to start with a company, partnership or company plus trust. These structures, company or company and trust will keep personal assets separate if ever a client or other publisher takes you to court. If a writer and just starting out, then you need to consider your writing income level and to minimise expense, the structure could be sole trader (sole entity) or partnership.

Remember to review this structure as your business grows and you start to take on higher-level projects and contracts. Never take on celebrity clients without reviewing risk.

LawPath or Sleek help you set up a company structure online for $597, covering ASIC registration and documents. Including setup, ASIC fee, compliance, and the years' accounting, you can get your company underway for as little as $1,677 (a discounted special at Sleek). Or you can seek your own accountant, with the average charge being about $1,200 for the end of year returns and Profit & Loss. Expect much higher costs for Trusts.

Read *The Journalists' Guide to Media Law*, M Pearson, M Polden (5th/ 6th ed.).

Insurance

As a nonfiction writer/publisher, you might need coverage against defamation. This would only protect you and your subcontractors, not your clients. They need their own insurance, if warranted. Professional Indemnity Insurance is the most needed for publishers and ghost writers, however there are other insurances which your insurance broker can help ascertain the need for. I use Bizcover (Australia), if this helps as a starting point.

Bookkeeping

Yes, you'll need to keep accurate records of invoices, receipts, banking, PayPal, and any requirements of your country and company, such as BAS quarterly accounts if you charge GST here in Australia.

Shoeboxes are out; software-as-a-service is in. Cheapest is Reckon at $22 per month normal rate for small business. Next is Quickbooks Simple Start (online), which is $29 per month. This price ignores the introductory offer, as that soon goes and it reverts to standard rates.

Use the Profit & Loss reports quarterly to keep track of what's happened, and the Cash-Flow Forecasting (or Budgets) to put in an estimate of what Income and Expenses are coming up.

One of the top reasons that small businesses go out of business is oversights in cash-flow planning, so don't let this happen to you!

Beg, Hire or Learn These Production Skills

You will need to consider the skills you have on tap. Daughter a graphic designer? Wife who's good at proofreading and (with time) editing? You're good at talking to clients about their goals and coming up with suitable quotes or packages? These are the kind of skills you need to acquire, have on tap or contract out. Usually in the case of editing, you would talk to two or three varied editors, both copy and developmental editors who can work under your brand and deliver good work.

As a micro publisher and editor, I believe editing is one of the most crucial skills to know about. Readers cannot hope to enjoy a book that jumps all over the place, that doesn't flow and that has needless repetition. This is developmental or structural. Some people will take great joy in pointing out every little copy error, such as missing words and apostrophes in wrong places. This is copy editing. Now with all the grammar editing tools, you as publisher can check your new editor's work in a rudimentary fashion. Ignoring some of the wrong markers of passive voice from the app, it can pick up elementary copy errors and things like double words or missing words.

If you want to hone your editing skills yourself, get yourself a subscription to Grammarly or ProWritingAid. It offers comprehensive grammar and style checking, along with detailed reports on writing style, readability, and more. You can also check how many times a writer has said a particular word and assess the number of glue (filler) words. Start by working on your own books and look up grammar rules as you go.

Also get a Style Guide (e.g. Strunk & White) and work up a simple style guide for your publishing house in order to maintain consistency. I use *The Australian Editing Handbook*, but it covers far more than you'll ever need.

Ensure Pages are Beautiful

Page layout – called typesetting – is another nicety to learn. As a strategic publisher, you'll probably choose to outsource this hefty time-consumer to a freelance book designer. There are plenty of good ones and an equal number of poor ones. So, ask for a pre-made typesetting sample that shows what they can do. Here are some things to check:

- Ensure that the leading (line spacing) is adequate.

- Does the typeface match the style of the book? What is it 'saying' to you? E.g. classic and worldly; modern, bold, creative.

- Does page numbering start in the right place?

- Are margins adequate for binding? A little more inside margin is a good idea.

- How do they treat images or tables and is there a caption system for tables/ figures?

- Do chapter starts have breathing space – and do they have a little flair?

The Low vs High Content Debate

Would-be micro publishers want to know: should I go with low content (journals, drawings, colouring books), medium content (20-25K words), or high content books? (Low content that is not up to par is being cracked down on by KDP and is outright not approved at IngramSpark).

To meet a market need, folk ask: what's the minimum page count that works for a book to be 'HIGH CONTENT'? Because this is the wrong question, there is no precise answer. Let's stop thinking like a schoolchild writing an essay and start looking at how business-minded authors attract, create massive value and maintain reputation. Let's also see how some use sales page offers to make book sales, while others utilise the Press and reviewers.

Russell Brunson has been very successful in both bookselling (both private and Amazon) and digital marketing. His landing pages reflect his prowess in copywriting, video and product offer creation. The three books in the Russell Brunson Secrets Trilogy Box Set—DotCom Secrets, Expert Secrets, and Traffic Secrets—define specific ways for a marketer to master sales funnels, using internet marketing, personal brand, and routing web traffic to offers. With hardback and a full set, the value for those struggling to get enough customers is off the charts. (View at: *https://secretstrilogy.com/get-the-trilogy-now?*)

Brunson's initial 'Traffic Secrets' funnel page asks you to choose between a 'free' book (shipping only) or buy on Amazon for $24.95. Sounds pretty good value! Brunson doesn't need to have a big upsell on the back end of that page. Plus, affiliates market it, so there's no ad costs. And all the freebie taker people, on email prompting, could buy the boxed set. But, wait, there's one more.

'Unlock the Secrets' (book #4) was the obvious title choice for the hands-on workbook. It brings all the other three book concepts together in one 614-page workshop-in-a-workbook to learn how to implement all kinds of sales funnels.

Unlock the Secrets is huge: covering a deep level of knowledge, strategy and detail that folks can use to learn and implement funnels. Starting in 2019, Unlock the Secrets became an event for ClickFunnels, where Russell Brunson and his team of mentors worked with participants to implement a sales funnel.

Whereas the first book was ostensibly free, this last book is only available with the full hardback set, sold for US$127. Yes, that's right, the four books are $127 (~AU $200).

So, this is a lesson in how to build value and create excitement. It's not about the number of pages or even the platform it's sold on; it's the value perceived by the intended target audience. Make sure your audience is hungry for what you offer and you are excited to give it to them.

Jennifer Lancaster

30

6

Suggested Budget Breakdown

The first budget breakdown is based on a digital first method, as there are higher risks and costs involved in print proofs and bookstore distribution. We want to go into business and stay there, with a realistic and viable budget.

You can still opt for paperbacks and hardbacks, utilising print on demand and their orders.

You perhaps might also do a budget for the year from your company's perspective (which really could be anything) but here it's easier to create a budget designed to return income based on each book published.

Research suggests that most small publishers put out 8-12 titles per year. But is that small press – or cooperative publishers who all work together? In the novice stage, I would suggest five titles in the first year, if you can secure some assistance.

It is important that your assistance is (preferably) known to you and lower cost than expert freelancers from our country. You can't be paying AU$90-$120 per hour for freelance book designers if you are to replicate your process and keep up the production schedule. On the other hand, cheaply designed and thrown up book covers don't sell at all, so a happy medium is needed. In authors' groups, 'Get Covers' has a good reputation for fixed fee fiction covers.

If one of you is good at graphic design, then you can make paperback covers in InDesign, with the aid of a cover template from IngramSpark's Resources to help see the spine guidelines and barcode. While some designers charge $1,500 per dust jacket, with the revisions they cover, your business needs trimmed costs. Two expert book designers in Australia charge AU$360 per cover, with three mockup designs, and one in Portugal charges US$200 (~$300) for print and ebook, with all the artwork. I am quite fussy about book covers, and these people's covers make the grade. A lot don't.

Allow a little for photography, illustration, or stock photos if wanted. You can manage quite well without. As a regret, poor cover design ranks up there with soap-on-a-rope for a treasured Dad at Xmas.

For a one-sheet, download my Expected Costs of Publishing at *https://jennifer-lancaster.com.au/report-thank-you/*.

Digital-First Small Publisher Cost Analysis

Per-Book Production Costs in AUD: Direct Costs

1. Editorial Services (AU prices)

- Developmental editing: $2,000–3,500 (not always needed)

- Copy editing: $1,400–1,900 (40,000 words)

- Proofreading: $400–600

(See overleaf for explainers)

2. Design & Production

- Cover design: $50-$150 (eBook and 3D)

- eBook Design potentially: $0-$70 (example .64 x 110 = $70) or use a tool like Atticus, etc.

- ISBN (through free option or bulk purchase): $0-25

3. Production Format Costs

- Print-on-demand setup: $0 (changes after 60 days: $45)

(ISBN Services.com charges US$69–89: ebook conversion for simple non-fiction)

4. Essential Marketing

- ARCs (digital subscription): $0-100

- Online advertising (Amazon Ads, Facebook): $500-1,500

- Virtual launch events: $100-300 for ads and giveaways

- NetGalley listing: $200 (shared package with a partner, e.g., BooksGoSocial).

Expected reviews: 6-15 per book launch

5. Staff Costs

- Project manager: your wage if you do it

- Contracted marketing support: ~$600 per title (or your wage)

Digital Approach Totals: $2,675–$4,800

Our example uses digital total: AU$3,375

Break-Even Point

At a price of $5.99: Break-even analysis (eBook sales) after GST (AU sales)

- Net revenue per sale from KDP: $3.77 AUD

- Copies needed to break even: **895** eBooks, but more likely, a mix of both print and digital revenue, e.g. half and half.

Total Costs for Digital and Print combined, example:

Without developmental editing: $4,470 AUD

With developmental editing: $6,670 AUD

Estimated Print Book Sales Needed to Break Even
(Assuming a 60% royalty after platform fees)

Book Price (AUD)	Sales Needed (No Dev Edit)	Sales Needed (With Dev Edit)
$14.99	561 copies	880 copies
$19.99	420 copies	660 copies
$25.99	340 copies	534 copies

The royalty takes into account 5% withholding tax taken out. This is what Australians who have done a tax interview and claim the US Tax Treaty pay.

Adding developmental editing increases costs, requiring more sales to recover your investment. Figures used the lower end of dev. editor rate.

Here's the process you need for more ROI Estimates:

1. Calculate the median cost for each service and cost
2. Sum up the total investment needed for publishing, incl. marketing.
3. Determine royalty per book = Book Price × Royalty Rate
4. Determine the number of book sales required to break even (based on the price point and royalty given). **Total Costs ÷ Publisher Royalty per copy = Sales Needed.**

Australian prices. Pro copyediting per word (nonfiction): $0.03 to $0.05 per word. There are all manner of editors so you'll want recommendations or testimonials. Developmental editing prices ranges from $0.07 to $0.10 per word or hourly rate of $50 to $150 per hour. Only ask for proofreading once editing and layout has been done.

Manuscript Appraisals can be one way to get professional advice in a report without the extra time from on-page suggestions. The editor reads through and suggests consistency elements, improvements in patterns or flow, and structure changes. These are from AU$400 to $1500+ (top end for lengthy books).

US prices. Developmental editing for nonfiction and fiction generally takes 4–6 pages an hour (avg. 1500 words), so if an editor has an hourly rate of $50, then a nonfiction book of 50,000 words may take a Dev Editor 33 hours + 2 hours communication.

Amazon Marketing Strategy

1. Amazon Marketing Services (AMS)

   - Average cost per click: $0.40-0.80

   - Typical conversion rate: 8-12%

2. Review Generation

   - Promotion via author app or network, expected reviews: 12

   - Organic review rate: 1-2% of sales

   - Target: 20-25 reviews threshold, for improved visibility

Additional Revenue Opportunities

1. Kindle Unlimited/KENP earnings: $0.004-0.005 per page read (amounts vary)

2. Expanded distribution through IngramSpark: Additional 15% market reach

3. Direct sales through publisher website: Higher profit from each book

KENP: The share of the KDP Select Global Fund allocated to each country varies based on factors such as exchange rates, reading behaviour, and local subscription pricing. Author earnings are then determined by their share of total pages read.

OverDrive is a library borrowing partner where the earnings would potentially be better, being that library prices you set should be 30-50% higher, however there may be fewer sales. Authors who distribute their books through Over-Drive, either directly or through a third-party aggregator, receive 50% of the

USD library price for each e-book checkout. (Draft2Digital is an easy gateway to Overdrive and Everand for those sales).

Some **Key Performance Metrics** on Amazon.com:

- Average conversion rate from ads: 10-15%

- Typical review rate: 1% of sales (boost this – ask in book!)

- Review accumulation timeline: 2-3 months to reach 20 reviews

Prices are in AUD and may vary according to unique costs.

- Optimal price point for fiction: **$2.99-7.99** (ebook), $15.99-19.99 (paperback)

- Optimal price point for nonfiction: **$3.99-9.99** (ebook), $17.99-24.99 (paperback), $29.99-37.99 (hardback)

- Optimal price point nonfiction AUST: **$4.99-9.99** (ebook), $21.99-29.99 (paperback).

Suggested prices unless very long and high resolution quality. Royalty rate changes at >$10.00.

Note: Amazon KDP is prone to re-price your paperback book at any point.

Print-First Approach (Extra Costs)

Total Paperback-Specific Cost: approx. $700 AUD

· Net revenue per sale: $6.00 AUD

A focus on print first and on attracting library suppliers would include these as **cost of goods sold:**

Book Formatting and Design – costs for print cover artwork and internals – $800–$1300
Editor fees (already included in eBook)
ISBN cost each - $8.80, buying 10 = $88 (+ $55 to set up account)^

Ingram global distribution fee: 1% of the list price for each copy sold
Some administration hours costed
Books + Publishing *Book Buzz* – Title Showcase listing# - $275
Facebook ads or Amazon ads if taken

If based in the US, then the Ingram magazine ad at US$80 each would be the equivalent, bookable through your IngramSpark/LSI account.

^ In the US, the ISBN cost is $29.50 each when buying 10.

In Canada or NZ, residents can register for an ISBN for free at their National Library.

UK residents pay £93 for each ISBN or £174 for 10 ISBNs through the Nielsen UK ISBN store. Ouch!

Library Supplier contacting is free. Just include a special price in your ISBN listing which is a little higher for these print copies (P&H is extra). Talk to local book acquisitions staff at networked libraries as well; they can give you more clues. Books + Publishing offer a weekly newsletter read by 40% of 8,000 industry subscribers, and the Title Showcase is for new listings only.

Australian Publishing Association Benefits:

APA membership gets you access to campaigns such as Australia Reads and discounts on the Australian Book Industry Awards and Educational Publishing Awards. With either Micro ($100 +GST) or Small Publisher ($250 +GST) membership, you'll also get advertising discounts and course discounts.

Professional courses include a potential editorial mentorship in Sydney, APA webinars, workshops, and access to the annual Bookup conference online (for $100 as a member). It's held in Melbourne in August.

https://publishers.asn.au/[Membership] - Associate Membership

Global readers, see: *https://www.allianceindependentauthors.org/*

For ongoing costs, there are a few to account for as a publisher. While you may not utilise all of these tools, it's funny how they add up after you set up your systems and processes.

Variable Budget for Micro Publishers

Software/Ass'n	Use case	Cost/month or Other
Adobe Indesign	Making books for IngramSpark	AU $29 – $39 pm
Quickbooks Simple	Bookkeeping	$29 pm for soloist
APA Micro or ALLi membership	Title visibility, Directory listing	APA $110 p.a. or ALLi US$119 (optional)
PublishDrive	Time-saving distribution	US$20.99 pm – 6 books (for example)
Kit.com	Email marketing and newsletters	$0 Newsletter plan <10,000
ProWritingAid	Grammar checking in bulk, export to Word	US$120 p.a. or see Info-Stack's annual offers for a great deal
SquareSpace	Website/Bookstore	$22–25 pm + 3% store transaction fee
Canva Pro	Social imagery, A+ images, book mockups	$16 pm or $165 p.a.
Stock Photos	Internals or website	($80 package at 123rf or Shutterstock)

Ghostwriters and Editors?

Now, some publishers are using AI writing and humanising services like Dibbly, however, this manuscript may need to be proofread by a professional editor on top of that. Be aware that readers get angry if they suspect that an author has simply pasted a chat response into their book. You also need to declare any AI generated content on loading at KDP. Dibbly costs US$1.70

per 100 words, but I don't believe that this is money well spent. If you don't get a professional editor after using a Chat program, then the voice and perspective will be all over the place.

To find an editor, look in your country's editor society or association. In Australia, it is the Institute of Professional Editors, however, bear in mind not every editor wants to pay to belong to such an association and pay extra for a directory listing.

Make a Valid Publishing Contract

Royalty agreements vary widely, and not all are created equal. To protect against liability and ensure fair compensation for authors, make sure your contract includes clear and specific royalty terms. Here are some key elements to look for:

1. Royalty Percentage

A royalty rate is the percentage one earns from book sales. In publishing contracts, different formats (hardcover, paperback, ebook, audiobook) often have different royalty rates. For example, in traditional publishing, eBooks usually have higher royalty percentages than print editions. They should not be lumped under a single rate but rather carefully thought through.

Industry-standard royalty rates range from around 10% (paperbacks) to around 50% (eBooks) but vary wildly in the hybrid world.

In addition, printed book overstock, thanks to the Amazon algorithm and their constant shipping, may cause prices and royalties to drop without your say-so.

2. How Royalties are Calculated

Understanding how royalties are calculated is critical. There are three common bases for calculation:

- **Cover Price (List Price):** Here, the royalty is a percentage of the book's retail price. This is usually the most favourable for authors.

- **Net Sales (Publisher's Revenue):** Royalties are based on the publisher's income after retailer and wholesaler discounts. Authors often don't get transparency.

- **Net Profit:** Royalties are based on what's left after the publisher deducts expenses such as production and shipping costs. This method often results in the smallest payout for authors and can be manipulated by the publisher.

✍ **Past Authors:** If you entered a contract where royalties were calculated based on 50% of net profit, this could be a warning sign. Hybrid publishers often take more split than is reasonable.

Ensure your authors know what their likely royalty is going to be, with a hypothetical example.

3. Clear Definitions of Terms

Vague or misleading terms in a contract can leave authors guessing. Insist on precise definitions of key phrases such as:

'Net Receipts': Typically means revenue the publisher receives after discounts and returns.

'Net Revenues': May include additional deductions like shipping, customs, and foreign sales costs.

'Net Income': Sometimes misleadingly used to mean 'net profit,' where expenses like printing and sales costs are deducted before calculating royalties.

For example, a fair definition of 'Net Receipts' might state: 'Revenue received by the Publisher from book sales, after discounts and returns.'

Before making a contract, consider carefully and seek advice from a publishing attorney. If you don't think through all expenses, they will punish your bottom line. Ensure the time window of publishing is reasonable as well.

4. Returns

In most bookseller cases, returns are deducted from authors' royalty account, but in the case of IngramSpark as distributor, publishers are 'charged the wholesale price of returned books back to the publisher (plus shipping and handling if the (US) publisher wants the book sent to them). Especially for a title with a lot of returns, it can be an expensive proposition.' (Source: WriterBeware Blog; 2024/12/06)

Ingram says on their blog that while online retailers are less concerned, 'typically, brick and mortar stores will not order a book unless it is returnable.' Publishers can choose for the book to be destroyed on return, saving the shipping and handling cost, which is $3 in the US. For Australians, they don't even offer returns-to-publisher as an option. (I've not had a problem with returns anyway).

If you change the price of your book, the charge for returns will be based on the wholesale price active in Ingram's system on the date the return is processed.

7

Markets, Not Marketplaces

Caxton showing the first specimen of his printing to King Edward IV at the Almonry, Westminster. Artist: Daniel Maclise. (CC) Wikimedia Commons.

It's Demand and Supply, Damn Fool!

William Caxton (c. 1422 – 1491) was an English merchant, diplomat and writer. He is thought to be the first person to introduce a printing press into England, in 1476. He printed many great Classics and some romance novellas and was perhaps the first English retailer of books. Evidently, he didn't translate languages very well but the early demand for French and Spanish books meant the press was kept busy.

Nowadays, there is a lot more supply than demand. Print on demand and self-publishing (with services) has opened the floodgates and all have come to make a penny or a pound. Two million books are published each year, globally, via the portals. That's why we have to think of markets, not marketplaces.

Market Strategy

The main problem when it comes to selling books is the promise of marketplaces as the only need. Promises of huge online distribution obscure the truth: that it's no good having titles on all the marketplaces without having a go-to-market strategy that attracts readers. It's also tempting to 'buy' a sale through advertising rather than build a brand and following over time.

So how do we define the right market strategy and market segment? If writing how-to or self-help, you must pick a problem before you even start the creation process. You should know generally what your 'book products' are the salve for, but don't stop there. Once you identify the right reader avatar, delve deeper into the reader's dream desires so that you meet these needs in the content of your books.

Always a solver of problems, notice that Alex Hormozi's books bring the attraction of the words '$100 million'. The hook for *$100m Leads* is: 'You can get 2x, 10x, or 100x more leads than you currently are without changing anything about what you sell'. Here, the problem is not having enough business leads, and the promise is results without sacrifice or lots of effort. Don't go promoting books with just the problem.

I put this idea into practice. I first wanted to write a book on all the publishing pitfalls, however, that is a negative thing. I thought about what the reader wants to achieve: a better publishing system. So, I changed it to *Set Up as a Micro Publisher*. My market segment is those who have published a book and are on their way to streamlining processes and being more successful at marketing. Those who desire a sideline business, knowing that building it takes skill, savvy, effort and reasonable time.

Many years ago, I noticed (with envy) how easy attraction seemed to be for a local author who wrote about quitting shopping for a year. People were lining up for her book. Though I don't remember her name now, the title was a clear winner. It's also a theme publishers love. 'My Year of No Shopping' was a break-out hit for Ann Patchett (New York). 'Not Buying It: My Year Without Shopping' (2007) was pretty good (73 reviews) too. 'The Year of Less' got 5,673 Amazon reviews. Not knowing any of this, in 2006 I wrote a short eBook, *How to Kick Bad Spending Habits*. I thought, 'hey this publishing thing is easy' as multiple sales rolled in (since they were new, Lulu provided the conversion). It was the theme (and cover), and not my genius that was a clear winner.

'People don't want to buy a quarter-inch drill. They want a quarter-inch hole.'
— *Theodore Levitt, Harvard Business School Professor*

Alternative Marketing Strategies

It's useful to find authors who sold in novel ways, as it can give you better ideas and rough guidelines you could use to promote and sell your line of books.

1. Richard Fenton & Andrea Waltz's - *Go For No*

Instead of selling their book one-by-one, they created bulk sales forms targeted at businesses, non-profits, and teams. These forms allowed companies to buy large quantities of the book at a discounted price.

Why it worked: The book has a strong message for salespeople and businesses, so entire teams or companies could benefit from reading it. Companies often buy in bulk when they see value in distributing a book to employees.

Result: They sold over 400,000 copies this way—many more than if they relied only on individual sales. Instead of selling a single book per time, they focused on selling 10, 50, or 100 books at a time.[5]

Another idea is to utilise a conference that attracts a niche type of professional and sell a book of interest in bulk to the conference organisers. Do not give your book away! They are the ones doing the goodie bags.

2. James Clear's 3-2-1 Email List for *Atomic Habits*

James Clear built a loyal audience with his 3-2-1 model newsletter:

- 3 ideas from him (usually related to habits and personal growth)
- 2 quotes from others
- 1 question to reflect on

Why it worked:

- It's consistent and easy to read, so subscribers looked forward to it every week.
- Over time, his email list grew to millions of people.
- Whenever he mentioned or promoted his book in the emails, many readers were ready to buy because they trusted him and loved his helpful content.

Result: His newsletter became a major driver of long-term sales for *Atomic Habits*, keeping it on bestseller lists for years.

Both methods are about leveraging relationships and trust, either through targeting businesses for high-volume sales or by consistently nurturing a large audience with valuable content.

James Clear got Penguin Random House to publish his first book. After realising that his millions of sales did not mean he had any rights to more of a cut or rights to the book itself, he founded 'Authors Equity', a publishing house giving their authors a larger cut of the pie and more creative control. This system is called 'author owned publishing', which is a bit higher level than general 'self-publishing'.

You might know an area already or be looking for a narrow niche. There are many tips on 'creating' a category and using language to attract a market in the eBook Snow Leopard. These authors, who came up with Ship 30 and Category Pirates, are the experts.

Memoirs or Biography – a Little More Humble

If writing a memoir, your market strategy might entail narrowing the stories towards a theme. You can see how professional writers do this in the biographies and ghostwritten memoirs in the bestselling books today. Check out your local library.

For biographers, you could do a Psychographic study. A psychographic study of a person is the analysis of their interests, opinions, and activities to understand what influences their behaviour. This is a lens through which you make the theme. A book about Andy Warhol's attitude to fame is more selective than a biography of his life and so can be made to stand out.

What Influences Book Buying?

One thing about target markets is they make the rules: it's no good targeting truck drivers if 90% of them don't read books. You need a hungry crowd of people who read. Take me for example. I've got 100+ books and 55 audiobooks, but there is always something new I'm itching to buy and read. (Although buying is a commitment I don't make lightly).

When it comes to promotional campaigns for specific titles, the AR survey found it is word-of-mouth that mostly influences the decision to buy, followed by publicity, then advertising, and then catalogues. Interesting to note, Shawn Coyne from Story Grid tells on his YouTube channel that authors who give away more books (like 1,000) seed and inspire this word of mouth, and the results take a long time. His example, a strangely titled book by Donald Miller, didn't reach #1 NYT bestseller but achieved consistent sales over two years.

Word-of-mouth works when the book written with a fresh voice and is nice to read. People enjoy it and tell friends; blogger enjoy it and write about it.

The top three factors that positively influence Australian readers when buying books are:

1. Previous enjoyment of book by same author

2. Recommendations of family & friends

3. Descriptive blurb on inside flap/back cover (not including cover review quotes or endorsements, which showed the lowest influence.)

Reading Patterns

There are fewer readers, but not because of clear reasons. Many people in Australia drive; a few take the train to work. An 'Australia Reads' survey says the number of book readers have dropped from 92% in 2017 to 75% in 2021, which is lower than countries like UK and Germany, both big on train travel.[6]

Audiobooks are more popular in Australia among adults, probably as they are easier to multi-task with, and 12% of Aussies buy their books online. That said, apparently 32% of Australians said they consider reading a hobby, compared to 44% in Spain and 42% in the UK.[7]

Do Kids Read Anymore?

With 90% of children pursuing screen-based activities, slightly less are reading books. According to recent data in Australia, 72% of children (aged 5-14 years) participated in reading for pleasure (down from 79% in 2017-2018). Reading for pleasure skews to the younger than 12 age groups. Of this 72% proportion, 32% read for 2 hours or less per week while only 2% read for 20 hours or more per week. In comparison, 40% of 5-14 year olds spent 10-19 hours per week on screen-based activities and 24% spent 20 hours or more weekly on their screens.[6]

Around 40% of Gen Z read a few days each week. Although most Gen Z prefer to read paperbacks over eBooks when they buy, particularly romance, fantasy and horror, 83% also turn to online sources like webnovels and ebooks for greater story diversity. (Wattpad, 2023).[1]

Ins and Outs of Audiobooks

Matt Tomporonski learnt about audiobooks while planning his launch of 'Letting Go Right Now'. He said: 'Unlike Amazon's print books, Audible sets pricing based on your audiobook's length. I aimed for the $19.95 US price point, which required a minimum five-hour runtime. I planned ahead and let my producer know I'd add content if needed to hit this threshold. Fortunately, the final recording came in at 5 hours and 45 minutes, comfortably securing my target price bracket.'

About 30,000 words is equal to 3.2 hours. The higher royalty payment structure favours audiobooks with a runtime (finished audio time) of greater than 3 hours, but there are many rules around exclusivity to Audible (higher royalty, around 50%) and whether it was sold to Audible members (almost half the royalty). ACX has stated:

> For audiobooks under 1 hour, your audiobook price will be less than $7.
>
> For books of 1 to 3 hours, your audiobook price will be $7 to $10.
>
> For books of 3 to 5 hours, your audiobook price will be $10 to $20.
>
> For books of 5 to 10 hours, your audiobook price will be $15 to $25. $19.95 seems to be a pretty common price in this range.
>
> For books of 10 to 20 hours, your audiobook price will be $20 to $30.
>
> For books of 20 to 30 hours, your audiobook price will be $25 to $35.

Audible Gate (Colleen Cross) in 2021 ousted Audible as not adhering to their own royalty rates. A $19.95 'exclusive' book was getting, in effect, about a 21% royalty, or $4.15 per member sale. A $19.95 non-exclusive book was getting, in effect, about a 13% royalty, or $2.59 per member sale. Authors were making even less for non-exclusive books not listed directly. (Source: *https://danieljtortora.com/blog/acx-audiobook-royalties-get-paid*)

In addition, you need to have audios in chapters, audio quality to be good, and other specific details that means it often requires assistance to get an audio-book through the process.

8

Marketing

There is a lot of work in planning and marketing. Further, many literary types distrust or feel misaligned with marketing, so they find it hard even when they know they must do it. So, let's keep things simple.

The most useful and relevant marketing is, according to the indie authors:

1. Their own email newsletter list

2. Review seeking – pre- and post-launch. (*See also* Market Secrets)

3. Using a designed One-Sheet and send to podcasters, bloggers, small media outlets.

4. Fantastic cover design (with photorealistic mockups) can help along your marketing efforts.

~

Google Your Book Title with your Name

Do you (the author) have a fancy Google page presence? In July 2023, Google implemented a substantial update, referred to as the 'Killer Whale', which increased the number of person entities within the Knowledge Graph. Knowledge Graph is their word for author description and links to books/work.

This expansion was aimed to enhance Google's ability to assess Experience, Expertise, Authoritativeness and Trustworthiness (E-E-A-T) for content creators, especially writers and authors. (Source: SearchEngineLand.com)

Tip: If you find a book that's not yours associated with your knowledge panel, then on that book, look to the right to 'Send Feedback to Google', take a screenshot and tell them it's not your book.

If you upload an eBook to Google Books (Play), they now make it available freely as a preview to all, with a link to buy. If you don't want everyone to be able to search and to read it, then I suggest don't upload it to Google Books.

Go-To-Market Plan

The Go-To Market Plan starts with a product. Your current product is a book, one of many perhaps. The way to do a market plan is to identify your niche market segment, make your product as professionally as possible, and then create strong messages so your 'product' stands out and resonates with this audience.

Use your unique ISBN to connect your title to the format rather than get free ones tying the publication to the KDP platform. It's easier to publicise with paperback, ePub and hardback unique ISBNs you buy yourself (via Thorpe/ My Identifiers). When you do this, you'll need to also fill out the form at the National Library and send the eBook version to them later to fulfill the legal deposit requirements. You usually need to send the print book to the State Library too.

The reason I mention this now is because of online visibility and the fact that an ISBN properly filled out will tie it to the publishing imprint, to author, and be listed in Nielsen Book Database.

If using IngramSpark or Lightning Source, you will also have library suppliers as a partner. Just to be doubly sure, I check my library price as well as email the spreadsheet of titles to James Bennett and Peter Pal, two library suppliers

(NSW). The library supplier ALS has their own sheet. Library suppliers and local libraries are buyers and it's best not to ignore them.

Now, let's go through some organic marketing options for your new Go-To-Market plan. Start your launch activities four months BEFORE publication date, then continue for around three months plus afterward. There is no reason for leaving your marketing activities aside till well after, as you can always make a gap between final edits of the manuscript and the launch date. This is what traditional publishers do, and while you don't need 12 months like them, two-three months after editing is ideal.

Marketing Tasks by Timeline

4 months before Publishing

Get well-lit author photos (e.g. for Goodreads and Amazon author accounts)

Order cover design (GetCovers, Red Raven, Fiverr)

3 Months before Publishing

Design or order various author banners for Facebook/LI featuring new book cover (3D)

Finalise book description

Finalise proofread of draft, receive all feedback.

2 Months before Publishing

Update all social media presences: make Facebook profile Professional and LinkedIn 'content creator' and set up a YouTube account.

Send proofread copies to industry pundits or peers for an endorsement.

Write on Substack and share sneak previews of your book chapter one. Add emails of friends and peers.

1 Month before Publishing

- Start writing book messages (curiosity-invoking hooks) – great for social updates & interviews.

- Join a review & newsletter swap site. Find other authors from your LinkedIn 1st connections and ask for a quick read-review of your coming book.

- As your book will be typeset by now, order a proof.

- Post a photo of you with early proof or gift copies ordered at Amazon.

- Follow up with an order of final, high-quality copies. Determine giveaway numbers.

- Optional: Design and order print bookmarks with correct buy URL.

- Seek podcasts and radio shows to go on to talk about book.

- Notify Library Suppliers (anytime before or after launch).

Launch Days

- Reduce eBook price to get many readers and encourage reviews on social media.

- Claim book and load your Amazon Author Central extra reviews or other bio details.

- Post a short video receiving the box of books. Tag @IngramSparkauthor

Post Publishing

- Write for a local street magazine and share your publishing experience, mention book! Write short reviews for book to submit to online booklover sites.

- Go on the publicity trail and craft a press release or SourceBottle pitch (don't pay for PR)

- Create a nice backdrop featuring your book (free digital background on Zoom)

- Always have your printed book in the background of video interviews.

- Give a quick shout out about others' related books – also note to them that you have a book and would love a shout out on socials or book review at some point.

Pleasing Your Market

To get a toehold in the marketing, we must focus more on pleasing our small sector of the market than on the great amorphous mass of book retail sales. The questions to investigate are:

✓ From research, what are my target readers eager to achieve or issues they need to solve? (Make notes)

✓ What words would they respond to, starting with what words they use in their favoured book reviews?

✓ What did my first readers say about the book's general usefulness?

✓ What specific demographics and interests do my researched readers share?

✓ Is there another target readership I have overlooked? e.g., a simple explanation of climate change could also work (with illustration) as juvenile non-fiction.

✓ What images would my target demographic respond to?

Test various types of images in ads or on social media posts. One cover I saw was so offputting I could not stand to even look at it. Only user testing will tell which is best.

Part 1: Making Stories

You need your online content to stand out, both articles and short social updates (and FB ads). If desired, use a Large Language Model to create a first draft only, not the whole thing – and iterate with your own story. There is a lot of dull content out there – but your stories and inside tips make it 'great'.

The kinds of stories are:

- Latest research applied in a person's reality
- Your inciting incident – what set you off on this path, was it a criticism or an accident?
- Your life turning point – what led you to write the book? What struggles you went through to even finish?

Remember, when making new posts, presentations and articles, put the emotion first.

How to do this at scale?

Using IdeaApe, it takes only a little time to research and collate thousands of people's real stories and problems from Reddit, into topical groups. (IdeaApe.com).

You may as well use your storytelling and observation skills to tell short pieces that inform and intrigue your social audiences.

Part 2: Making Images

It's not about making some futuristic image, no siree, we need to create imagery that connects on a deeper level. So, the most engaging is clear, bright pictures of you doing things (not in a studio). The second most engaging is three-dimensional images of your book. You do this by uploading your flat book cover to Canva, then popping it into a grid frame inside a template. Or you can use the 'Mockups' app or predetermined mockups in there.

If you're not into playing there, you could alternatively use Place-it.net to retrieve done for you mockups -- images of your book in different settings. It costs around US$8 per image though.

Bluesky, X or Threads?

You might prefer to avoid or leave X these days. While the newer *Bluesky* platform resembles Elon Musk's X, with a 'discover' feed and a chronological feed for accounts, it is decentralised, meaning users can host their data on servers other than those owned by the company. Bluesky initially attracted renegade journalists and writers and now is attracting others but is still small.

Threads attracts novelists, health & fitness types, life coaches and other writers. If you have an Instagram account, you simply join/log in with that, so that part's easy. Posting boring stuff is no good here, you have to make conversation and tell a story, sometimes with your own pictures.

Press Pitches

What online news is grabbing your attention the most? Those news publishers are not daft; they know how to write a headline. You must learn how to too. No, you don't need an expensive course on PR and publicity. But you do need to focus on timeliness. This means aligning your story with current events and trends. A timely and newsworthy pitch has a sense of urgency that can make it more appealing to journalists.

The main thing to remember is that pitching a story is not a static thing; it's more of a zig-zagging line of steps. What you need is a short article/piece (250 to 300 words) that brings to light some interesting fact that clearly relates to your latest book's subject. For instance, say your book is about being a mum of twins – your pitch highlights how mums don't always get any holidays – timed for Mother's Day. A new take on an existing resonant theme.

Remember to research the outlet's reader demographics and lifestyle interests.

Here are the steps to pitch editors or at SourceBottle, where you don't need to find the editors' addresses (sourcebottle.com):

Step 1: Headline
Come up with a headline that will appear like a swan among pigeons; one that doesn't mention either 'book' or 'launch'.

Step 2: Opening line

Come up with a summarising yet sparky opening line. What is the story offering in juiciness?

Step 3: Components of a press release

Hone your press release story, add contact details, include a picture (adding 'high resolution images available through XX'), add the date of release, etc.

Step 4: Editor List

Get a VA to track down 50 editors' or journalists' addresses in your country, with a focus on the field you specialise in or the locale you live in. At this stage, determine whether you are only pitching an experience or quote (like in HARO or SourceBottle) or if you are providing the story elements.

Step 5: Pitch story

Pitch, adding the story to the email to send to each editor. Track this sending in a simple spreadsheet. Try not to add attachments on the first email.

Step 6: Follow up

Follow up the pitch after 7 days (phone is best but this might not be discoverable).

I forgot to start with why you want to pitch. You want to pitch or send a story to editors, journalists and notable bloggers because this is how you get stories written about your expertise and, if you're the expert in the subject, about your book. If you've written for RELEVANT magazines before, do send those people the story idea first.

Distribution: If doing it yourself, you can choose to subscribe to MediaNet, AU$350/month for three months (account can be shared), or just choose the defined media lists you want to send to, for an ad hoc approach. (Plans: *https:// www.medianet.com.au/plans*). Starting with the free plan, you can create a press release with their easy compiler. Also check the 'events' calendar for special days that are coming up, to work in with those. If you don't buy a list or have a list yourself, there won't be much point in doing the release just to sit on a website news feed.

Journalists prefer to work with those they know and can see value in. List of Melbourne/Sydney events where you can meet the media:

https://www.medianet.com.au/meet-the-media

Making Expo Stalls

If you're like me, i.e. cheap, you will only be exhibiting your books at $20 or $30 stalls for indie authors or perhaps setting up a table at a market. (You could also ensure you are popping your book out when networking). Making a few things can make your books and stand 'pop', and some don't cost much at all.

- Tablecloth in brand colour: $8 piece from fabric store, sew under hems
- Bookmarks, classic/gloss: $41 for 100 + freight (BannerBuzz)
- Banner, tall, roll-up: about $110 - $150
- Bowl with a card-entry draw for a lucky door prize: cost of prize
- Book easel (stand): $11-$19.75 (Raeco, standard; AliExpress for larger)

9

Marketing Secrets and Optimisation

Publisher Website

Organic Traffic, Yes Please

Your number one idea to perennially promote books and services is likely: design a website and cash in on unpaid traffic on Google. You're a genius! There are certainly ways to capitalise on search engine seekers for a publisher or author website, but no tactic comes without work! People will generally find your website through a combination of author name and book title or perhaps for your niche.

You can seed direct visits by having your website address and a fun call-to-action emblazoned on your author/publisher business card.

Google isn't the only source of free visitors; there is also Facebook, Instagram, YouTube and LinkedIn. However, folk often won't click through to your website to find out more. Happy as a clam on FB or Instagram, they often don't move away. Whereas, with a Google search, some will click on a top ranked site... unless there is an AI answer right on the search results page. (An informational search). ChatGPT and Pinterest can also potentially send traffic.

You need to find out where these visitors have come from. It may be surprising to find out that social media sends very little traffic. You can also see which country they're from. You can find out all this with Google Analytics.

Some Benefits of Organic Visitors

The most obvious benefit: you are not paying directly for website visitors, although you might have spent on website design and store setup. The thing is, you will always pay something – including time – to have a viable bookstore website.

No matter if you try to use WordPress.com, SquareSpace or Wix, some upgrades will be needed if you want to capture emails. SquareSpace is a bit easier to manage for those not wanting the hosting, theme and plugin update headaches, as the host part is all taken care of.

Returning traffic is a boon for authors. If you don't have a decent email list, or else advertising, then your lovely website probably won't attract many return visitors.

One main benefit of a publisher website is to advertise and sell books directly. But remember that they will come for the blogs and reader magnets as well, to get to know you. The other benefit is to capture the emails of readers, something that Amazon KDP doesn't let you do.

If you prefer to use WordPress, the installable CMS, then go to Hostinger Web Hosts. They offer US$2.99/3.99 a month hosting with value-packed services. Hostinger also provide AI design, if you're pressed for money and want to achieve a website quickly. (I use this company for all my websites).

So, there are many benefits of attracting organic traffic, including 'kind of free' advertising to people typing in an author name or book titles, interesting them in subscribing to your engaging newsletter, and warming up potential readers with educational or witty articles.

1: Check out all Book Listings across all Retailer Sites

When you have checked out these sites, you'll notice that descriptions may be lacking some appearance qualities. In fact, it may need much more spacing, funky bullets, and sometimes the cover image is missing. While it's difficult to affect the retail end points, you can try to put <BR> in the HTML of a description on KDP/IngramSpark, etc, meaning a new line.

Check out most of your book listings at once with the book purchase site *Booko.com.au*. Check:

- Amazon.com.au, .com, .co.uk

- Goodreads.com – claim your own book by being an author there. Encourage book-loving friends to add it to their reading list. (Find friends on Goodreads first).

- Booktopia.com.au (Australian retailer)

- Kobo & Everand (subscription based)

Use this free description generator to make better book descriptions. See *https://kindlepreneur.com/amazon-book-description-generator/*

2: Get Reviews via Niche Bloggers

This tactic means being nice! After being helpful by pointing out something they could add for better monetisation, or rearrange, the blogger is more likely to pay attention. Find book bloggers or BookTokkers (on TikTok) who review books on your subject matter or genre. After a friendly reach-out in a FB or Tiktok message, you'll give each blogger a free ePub or paperback copy in exchange for an honest review. (Usually it's only on their website, so specify if you are seeking Amazon and Goodreads reviews).

Some people arrange a virtual blog tour over a week or two pre-launch, across multiple blogs. This means more people listing your book review or article. But you need to drill down on the types of bloggers interested in your books, which can consume enormous amounts of time. So, take the easier path and use a partner of NetGalley. I recommend BooksGoSocial or BookBuzz, as they offer even more book readers on top of NetGalley's listed book bloggers, critical reviewers and librarians.

Expert publisher Andrey says that he has more success with finding reviewers directly through networking, rather than using a tool. He says that one-third of those asked will give an Amazon or Goodreads review.

While you cannot pay for a review (except Editorial Reviews) you can make friendships with passionate readers/writers who would have bought this sort of book anyway. Sometimes reviewer tools can give you nonsense or trite reviews. You can build out your email list of interested readers (be sure to 'tag' them), ensuring that you directly ask for permission to send further emails.

According to Amazon rules, you are not allowed to pay a friend for a review or review swap. It's best to use gifting of eBooks direct through your author's Amazon listing (once logged in) but you must get them to put that the reviewed book was a gift.

It's a great idea to get at least five reviews on your retailer listings. For example, if using Booktopia, prompt first readers you know to go review on that site and give instructions to make it easy. If using Amazon.com.au, prompt the readers to go to the right marketplace and URL to review the book, and don't rely on chance.

Is it beneficial to get book reviews on individual creator's blogs?

Yes, it is beneficial in the launch period due to the creation of many articles (more eyes) and many links (more popularity) back to your main book selling website, whether that be your site or Amazon's.

3: Write Articles with Sales Page Links

This is where you write certain length articles at online magazines and news sites. If you're trying to rank better on a particular bookseller, it's best if your article links point there. But if you are writing for general credibility, then you'd link back to your own author/publisher website.

First, check the Submission Requirements, including if they give you a byline and allow a link in it to the book page. I found a huge list of magazines at a State Writers' Centre, those which let writers submit their articles, some digital and some print, where you can gather some credibility and perhaps mention your coming book. This does take time, so if you prefer talking instead, go down the Podcast Guesting route prior to or at launch.

4: Run a Reader Giveaway

I have done this before with some level of ease and reward. Ideally, it's best with a site that lets you collect email addresses – so you can tell them all next time you have written something amazing. The sites I've used are:

- StoryOrigin (US$10 per month) – create landing pages for reader magnets and group promotions
- BookFunnel (yearly or US$10 monthly)– mostly fiction writers
- Rafflecopter

Rafflecopter helps to run a giveaway and collect addresses. I paid $15 to have it look better when sharing my book competition link. Though we had a grateful winner, entry numbers weren't worthwhile. To empower your launches through the author community, perhaps it's better to have a tool like one of the others and only pay on launch months.

You could also do unofficial reader giveaways using Amazon, as it's easy to gift a book (at author price). Look up the KDP Help menu to find the basics. While you cannot run a 'giveaway' for Kindle books, you may be able to run one for your paperback book. Don't forget, you must log in first, using the username of your KDP account. You'll send the gifted books one by one to the winners. Then send them pleasant reminders to review via email.

For pre-publication ARCs not using a tool, you would need to order an author copy (logged into your KDP) then send on. With the likes of BookFunnel you send a digital book securely (ePub or PDF).

Goodreads still offers giveaways, but the price is now exorbitant (US129) and not worthwhile for most.

You won't be able to do any special activities like this for a book published through IngramSpark, except through your own social media, with the delivery systems above.

ARC = Advance Reader Copy. ePub = industry standard ebook format.

✋ Action Jackson

To start with a book review or giveaway, have everything ready.

- Your book cover, sales blurb, and formatted book should be complete, and links to review sites should be ready to share.

- Choose keywords that help your book stand out in Amazon search results. On platforms like Bookfunnel.com or Booksprout, keywords are essential for ensuring your book reaches the right audience.

5. Build a Community First

When you're listening to experts, take notes. Then, after considering your unique viewpoint, decide whether to use a tool for research or to listen to your intuition.

Category Pirates are a case study in building a community around their key messages, which led to consistent eBook sales… rather than two months of sales and then nothing.

Who are the Category Pirates?

The Category Pirates are a group of thought leaders in category design and creation, including:

Christopher Lochhead: A former CMO, Lochhead is a #1

Apple business podcaster and author. His first book, *Play Bigger*, is considered 'the bible of category design'.

Eddie Yoon: Yoon has written more about category design and creation for The Harvard Business Review than anyone else. He's the author of *Superconsumers* and runs 'Eddie Would Grow', a growth strategy 'think tank' and advisory firm.

Nicolas Cole: Cole is a serial writing entrepreneur and one of the most consumed digital business writers in the world. Having been a tippy top writer on Quora, he went on to tell his secrets in *The Art & Business of Online Writing*. He's the founder of Digital Press.

The reason these guys are different is because they already tried traditional publishing and eBooks, but getting together, they saw a new way to do paid publishing. Early adopters, they did it via Substack: offering subscribed readers 'mini books' and long promotional book previews. Rather than charge for their first co-authored book 'Category Design Toolkit', they gave the full book to paid subscribers.

'Some napkin math told us that getting (some) people to buy a $20 book is way less advantageous than getting a small percentage of those free readers to subscribe to our newsletter for $200/year' said Eddie Yoon (Interview: *https://on.substack.com/p/grow-series-19-category-pirates*)

Their publication Category Pirates hit #4 in the Business category in paid Substacks after one year of extraordinary growth, truly showing the power of four focused minds, including their editor. Substack takes a 10% commission.

I am not suggesting the same strategy could work for an unknown solo author who is not in the luxurious position of testing out long previews with all their hard work. However, it's worth considering a Substack early readers strategy – for one, it's a lot easier than a blog to run, and for another, some readers just happen by your newsletter on the Substack App.

There is also a thriving Substack writer community and the addition of 'Notes', a bit like X, to reach others. Also, you may net a small income in yearly memberships (offering good perks) once your readership is engaged.

6. Analyse Categories but don't Paralyse

There is a lot to be said for research before launching into a crowded space! Small publishers utilise Publisher Rocket or BookBeam tools to find categories and keywords that sell. Publisher Rocket now lets you put in an ASIN (the Kindle book number) of a top-selling competitor book, then you can then see what titles use what keywords and how much it sells. BookBeam also allows a reverse keyword search from a certain book's ASIN, which is one way to find good keywords. You want keyword phrases with low competition and a high number of searches.

A word on price. While there is a cost to these tools, many people fall for the trap of paying for a course. Save yourself thousands by diligently utilising the same tool again and again and viewing their included training videos. Dave Chesson and Dale Roberts have hundreds of free videos on YouTube as well.

Publisher Rocket is a one-off cost (now US$150). See *https://bit.ly/rockettool*

BookBeam does not allow searches in Amazon Australia, it has six marketplaces plus book tracking and Basic Plan is US$348 annually. Not recommended for Australians, except their 'lite' Chrome Extension. (*BookBeam.io*)

Competitor checkup: Dave Chesson also designed a free 'book sales calculator', where you can put in any book's Amazon bestseller rank to get a rough estimate of daily sales. *https://kindlepreneur.com/amazon-kdp-sales-rank-calculator/*

7. Paid Shortcut: Launch Tools

For growing social media pre-launch, a service called Thunderclap can be utilised if willing to pay. If you've left your social media presence to lag for years, this may be a good alternative to paid social media managers, although, as always, 'approach with caution'.

You can purchase follows on the platform you most want. (*Thunderclap.com*)

That said, you should not be paying various media (e.g., Readers Favorite Awards, X (Twitter)-based lists, BlueInk reviews, etc) for doubtful, unproven results. Business or literary magazines unknown to you charging $500 per feature and any author competitions with chunky fees... all fall in this same camp. The mantra 'metrics are sanity, followers are vanity' could apply here. Matt Stanton writes on LinkedIn:

'Vanity metrics are figures that make you feel warm and fuzzy inside, but don't really mean anything. They include the numbers of views, likes, and comments on your posts, and contrast with sanity metrics, which would be things like the number of direct inquiries about your services, the number of new customers you're getting, the value of the sales you're making, etc.'

With metrics in mind, pay-per-click ads and a focus on resultant sales numbers are a good way to go, as is getting verified reviews through your own people network. (Verified meaning the person has bought the book).

8. Advertising and Promotion: KDP

Successfully marketing your book on Amazon involves using the right tools available within Kindle Direct Publishing (KDP), some free and one paid. So many novices to book publishing don't use or test out these tools, not understanding that we need every tool for selling supplied to us!

Here's a step-by-step guide to finding and using these marketing tools effectively.

Accessing Marketing Tools in KDP

Once a book is published on Amazon KDP, you can access various marketing tools through the KDP dashboard:

Go to kdp.amazon.com and sign in.

In your KDP Bookshelf, select 'Marketing' from the top menu.

Explore Available Tools:

- Amazon Advertising: Create paid ads to promote each book.

- KDP Select Promotions: See below.

- Author Central: In the drop-down, select Amazon.com, then go find and add your new book. Make an edit here to add any prelaunch 'editorial reviews'. Write a short, snappy, credible author bio.

- Add A1+ content to display bullet list, 3D graphics and other testimony.*

- (Beta) Nominate a book for Prime Reads or Kindle Deals.

Author Note: For fan-building, the 'Follow' button on an Amazon author page is helpful. If you put out another book, an email will go to fans with the release information. You have set up Amazon Author Central, right?

*A1+ content can be made easily with a Canva template; email me for examples.

Benefits of Enrolling in KDP Select

KDP Select is an optional program that offers Amazon exclusive marketing benefits in exchange for a 90-day exclusivity agreement. If enrolled, it means you cannot then add the ebook to other portals, like Draft2Digital. But you can do on-site free and discounted promotions. Here's what you get:

Free Book Promotion (Once Per 90-Day Cycle)

- Make an ebook free for up to five days.

- Great for attracting new readers and increasing reviews, if you also promote this fact on Facebook groups or via paid eBook reader sites. (You must not upload the book at these sites if in Select, only the Amazon link).

- Kindle Unlimited & Kindle Owners' Lending Library

- Your ebook is included in Kindle Unlimited, where readers can borrow and read it.

- You earn royalties based on the number of pages read (KENP - Kindle Edition Normalized Pages).

Kindle Countdown Deals

- Offer time-limited discounts while retaining your royalty percentage.
- Countdown timers create urgency, boosting sales.

Increased Discoverability

- Books in KDP Select are more likely to be recommended by Amazon's algorithm.
- They appear in Kindle Unlimited recommendations, increasing reach. (However, payouts here are very low).

Author Follows and Engagement

When a reader downloads your book, they can follow you via Amazon's 'Follow' feature. Ensure you fill out your profile at Author Central.

Amazon notifies followers about your new releases, increasing future sales.

You can also nominate eBooks to be included in **Kindle Deals and Prime Reading** promotional programs to reach new readers. To be eligible for Kindle Deals, a title must be: an eBook listed already, not erotic, be listed from US 2.99 – 11.99 (US marketplace), not be discounted in last 30 days, be in the same language as the marketplace. For Prime Reading, the eBook must be enrolled in Kindle Select.

Enrolling in Amazon Ads (KDP Marketing Tab)

Amazon Advertising allows you to run ads that appear in search results and on relevant product pages, right from your KDP dashboard.

It is a good idea on launch to experiment a little with Amazon Ads. As you pay per click, if you have enough royalty to cover it then you can spare up to $0.80 per click... if your selling rate is something like 8 clicks to 1 purchase. You'd spend $6.40 to get a sale. You can see why the numbers are better for high-royalty paperbacks, if that's possible. If you're not getting the purchases, then you need to improve the blurb and get expert help on the ad/keyword process.

Here's how to set up an ad campaign:

1. Click on '**Amazon Advertising**' in the KDP Marketing Tab.

2. Choose an **Ad Type**:

    - Sponsored Products: Target keywords and categories to reach readers.

    - Sponsored Brands (available to authors with multiple books): Promote a collection of books.

3. Set a **Budget** and **Bid Amount**: Start small and adjust based on performance.

4. Select **Targeting Options**:

    - Automatic Targeting: Amazon selects relevant keywords.

    - Manual Targeting: You choose the keywords or books to target.

5. **Launch the Campaign** and Monitor Results: Track impressions, clicks, and conversions to adjust your strategy over time.

I would choose my keywords after doing two hours research of such. One hack: I use Keywords Everywhere, the Chrome extension where you can see the more popular keywords (drawing from Google search). But it has nowhere near the great research power of Publisher Rocket.

Another hack: use Amazon Suggest to find popularity. This means that when you type words into the Amazon window, the algorithm starts guessing what you mean. If something like ATOM is written, you can bet that it brings up ATOMIC HABITS.

There are AI-driven Amazon Ad managers, if you prefer that. *Publishing Performance* is one that operates as an Amazon Ads account manager. It selects and optimizes keywords, sets and adjusts bids automatically, and continuously refines campaigns to reduce ACOS, boost sales, and drive organic rankings.

It costs US$39/mth or $390/year. (*PublishingPerformance.com*, run by Teddy Smith).

9. Make Friends with Meta

Meta (Facebook/Instagram) Ads

If you use Meta ads and profit's your aim, you need to have either a high paperback royalty ($7 plus) or a business to secure upsells. It's good to set up a Meta pixel on your website a month ahead and start with about a $7-30 ad strategy (across 5 days) just to get the ads algorithm to start learning what content works.

It's best to invest in amazing design for your book ad, rather than rely on only the cover. Anyway, it needs to show in various sizes and starting from a square image is better. Consider using your face as well, for added traction. (Designers, see Canva.com – Facebook Ads canvas).

Meta Ads are best set up from Ads Manager.

Facebook Author Pages

Experimenting with posting on a publisher imprint page, views were nil, so I turned my Facebook profile into a Professional profile and put the background as my latest book plus message. Starting afresh in 2024, I easily built up 324 followers and 250 friends. (Two-factor identification is a must to prevent hacks).

Here, posts should be more 'natural' in nature (birthday, travel and pictures of you writing) and can include you talking on reels as well, which is great for visibility. The best performing reel last month regarding books was my personal request for feedback on what marketing people need, and I was holding up two of my books.

As a 'creator', your dashboard contains all the help and tools needed. In the dashboard, you can use Meta Business Suite's *Planner* to post a week's worth of content... but leave a spot or two for spontaneous photo shares.

There is a comments manager. You can see things you posted under 'Content'.

Also check out the Professional mode guide, which is under 'help and guidance' in the Professional dashboard. View insights about the age and gender of your audience and view the number of 'content interactions' on a 28-day basis. You can easily advertise from a professional profile too.

There, you can set up posting automatically on Instagram or vice versa, bearing in mind that square images and portrait short videos of <59 seconds look and perform the best for Instagram.

The background Facebook Cover photo size: minimum 851 x 315 pixels. You can select this type in Canva and then look at recommended templates. Upload your own book mock-up shot, with the same colours, and an inspiring message if appropriate.

Facebook Insights

You: the fresh social content maestro, need to monitor your results. Go to the Professional Dashboard of your Facebook author page. Check out the Content section. If using a Facebook Profile, turn on the Professional mode, upload a cover with publications on it, and you can Schedule posts in this profile too. Schedule for evenings or whenever friends are most active.

Professional Dashboard. While my Business Author Academy page got 34 views, recently my Professional Profile got 3,048 views and 12 comments, including of videos. I barely touched Stories, but I wrote on how hard the business and job struggle has been, posted a video asking for feedback, and pimped my personal publishing updates.

Look at what content has gotten the most traction and reactions. Do more of that!

10

The 'Cheap eBook' Strategy

It's always best to focus on quality and find a profitable niche first rather than rely on luck, price, and perfect timing.

We find a niche with the eBook research tools, e.g. Publisher Rocket, KDP Spy. While it's ever popular, the cheap eBook strategy is more about lowering prices to get reviews and sales, whereas I believe that creating insider content that people are looking for is the better strategy.

That said, many indie authors have already set up camp in their chosen genre and are battling it out for reader views with half a million others. Now that you know that, here are the tips if eBook sales is your sole intention.

About Kindle Select and their Deals and Promotions

While with the lower levels (0.99) you are set to break even at best, Kindle ebook promotions may be a good way to get your publishing imprint off the ground.

Question doing free eBook promotions, because these downloaders are unlikely to support authors and give reviews—unless you actually know them.

Most authors like the 99 cent promotion to launch with, as it's frictionless. It equals $1.49 in Australia. You will want to put up the average price after launch. After 30 days, offer other deals via the Countdown, Prime or other Kindle Select user options.

Ticking 'Select' in KDP means you're not ebook publishing elsewhere online. There are many rules; authors in the KDP Select program aren't allowed to share more than 10% of their book's content anywhere else, including blogs or other websites. Kindle Unlimited royalties are on 'per page read' and are very low. KU is popular with consummate readers, who borrow and give back books willy-nilly for one low fee.

The royalties aren't much to shout about, with 33 cents often appearing in my author accounts rather than the ~$2.00 for an eBook that they should get.

Free books (up to 5 days, on Amazon.com, co.uk only) might get new books up the levels in Amazon rankings – even to #1 in a category if you have tons of friends – but remember our goal: to make a profit long term and beget reader loyalty.

US-based Kindle Deals – in USD

Fiverr (@bknights service) – $8 to $25 – website/newsletter 5500 daily visits, 50,000 subs

BookSends – $60 – 120,000 subs

Ereader News Today – $25 to $150 – 150,000 subs

Books Butterfly – $50 to $600+ – 150,000 subs, guaranteed downloads

Just Kindle Books – $22 to $45 – News/home/social. 49,000 subs, 27,000 FB users (EReader Nation)

Freebooksy – $40 to $200 – recommending the Bargain Booksy part

The Fussy Librarian – $10 to $50 – 10,000 subs

Robin Reads – $60 to $120

(Just Google the exact name with 'book promotions' to find their page)

A test done by the crew at PaidAuthor.com of Books Butterfly, for US$50, utilising the Kindle Select allowance for 5 days of free ebook promotion, netted 1,700 downloads. They have promotions for free, 99 cent eBooks, and over $1 eBooks. Hard to say if it helped other titles sell from that deal.

If your focus is getting reviews, this service provides a money-back guarantee and accesses true book reviewers:

BooksGoSocial, an aggregator of NetGalley. The Starter US$99 package has a Giant email option to help get sales, or a NetGalley reader review option, or an Editorial review option. Books will need to have at least seven reader reviews already on Amazon to use the Giant email boost. (Mixed outcomes: 3.5 stars reviews.co.uk and 4 stars on Trustpilot).

If a paid member of ALLi, you also get a good Netgalley deal there.

Australian-Based Book Promotions

The **Australian Authors Marketplace** offers (besides a free listing) book promotion across their website and reader FB page.

One month: $15, Two months: $27. Front page promotion for one title, 2 x social media feeds, and link from your author profile on AAM. (*https://australianauthors.net.au/book-promotion/*)

Book Muffin works like Readers Favorite, except you are more inclined to gain Amazon reviews from the reviewer. As you join, you get muffin credits which you can use to request a review. With a lifetime fee of approx. AU$80, or a free 10-day trial, I gave it a go. There are not enough users at this stage but the team was gracious enough to review my book. You have as long as you want to do your reading and reviewing assignment of other books – but it pays to be a Kindle Unlimited member. I managed to find a couple books listed at about $1.50, so that was fine to review. They were both mediocre. Paying to get the author's book means that you give a verified review – and vice versa – so it's a valid idea. Not many book reviewers are attracted to this site.

Never mind. Ian Bosler suggests in his book, *Unlock Your Book's Potential:* *'Marketing isn't all promotion, rather promotion is a small but important element in your marketing endeavours.'*

Selling overstock or outdated books:

Try Suitcase Rummage market (sell from a suitcase), in Brisbane, Sydney, Melbourne. (*www.suitcaserummage.com.au/market-dates*) It's $30 + fee.

Book Promotion Requirements in Depth

BookRaid is a place using pay-per-click style advertising for eBook launches. They promise your campaign goes to their 50,000 reader list, people who want free and low cost eBooks. Reviews from authors have been mixed.

A book must meet the following requirements to qualify for a BookRaid promotion:

- Recently discounted by 50% or more. Or free.
- Not promoted by BookRaid in the last eight weeks.
- Available on Amazon.
- High quality titles, covers, and descriptions. Book content should have few or no spelling/grammar errors.

BookRaid click campaigns are way more affordable than BookBub Featured Deals. Although an author partner account is free to hold, BookBub only accepts around 5-10% of authors for their 'Featured deals'. For this an author needs several 4 and 5 star reviews and other professional markers. Some categories cost $750 to enter. For some, click results are abysmal.

BookRaid is a smaller outfit, where profits go back to growing the reader list. Their prices are:

- Free ebook promotions cost $0.15 per click (the aim is purely downloads)
- $0.99 promotions cost $0.20 per click - compare this to your Amazon ad costs for launches
- $2.99 promotions cost $0.60 per click
- Full cost is a maximum of $60 per campaign. (All prices are in USD).

Some prolific fiction authors recommend Freebooksy and Fussy Librarian as alternatives to BookRaid (included in the table). Written Word Media's

Freebooksy also offer a 'Bargain Booksy' promo, which is for eBooks from $0.99 to $5, does not require Amazon reviews (but is vetted), and pricing depends on category. (An example: pay US$40 for sending a self-help eBook to 200,000 readership).

> 'The main drawback of a service like this (Fussy Librarian) is the short-term revenue loss from paying for the service and decreasing the price of your book.' – BookLinker, 2023

Others prefer the control of **Amazon Ads**. Written Word Media also run Meta Ads and Amazon Ads for authors and this is tempting due to the complexity of setting it up yourself. 'Reader Reach' costs $135 - $150 per ad run, and data reaches out to a set of one million readers (based on their interests). Whether those click or buy is related to the book's magnetic attraction. (*https://www.writtenwordmedia.com/reader-reach/*)

Some authors use much more expensive 'author marketing experts' (circa $2,500) and again, many fall into traps. The offer of an easy advertising service can be appealing, but if an author calculates potential earnings based on realistic scenarios, they might find that selling X number of books at, for example, $1.50 profit each, is insufficient to cover the cost of the service plus advertisements. While the value of X is unknown, it's likely lower than they suggest, so use a logical judgement to assess if it's worthwhile.

Re-work the marketing plan until you reach a decent profit margin at a fair number of sales based on your past book sales or similar indie book sales, etc. Some in the Driven Publishers' Skool group suggest that $3 profit (ebooks) and $7-10 profit (print) is an ideal minimum for those who are utilising direct click advertising (with higher profits needed on Facebook). I tend to agree.

Let's look at a completely different perspective.

11

The 'Viral Message' Book Strategy

When you have a strong message, brand and positioning, your book has more chance of lift-off.

Book Positioning

A simple formula for how to position a book for a viral message is:

Viral Message = Clear Positioning + Relatable Story + Shareable Hook

Clear Positioning: Identify what makes your book unique and relevant to your target audience. It should address specific needs, desires or problems. I particularly like a PROMISE that relates to a PROBLEM.

Relatable Story: Craft a story that resonates emotionally with your audience, making them feel connected.

Shareable Hook: Create a tagline or idea that is easy for people to remember and share with others.

Promise: What are you saying the book will help them achieve in their life? It can indeed be an emotional pay-off.

When combined, these elements increase the chances of your book and its message spreading widely.

Positioning can be ascertained in the research phase, when you're seeing a gap in the market for a particular message or type of book. Some topics are crowded, such as leadership or marketing, and this is where clever positioning helps. Seth Godin, the genius at this, called his book 'This is Marketing'. Always fighting the idea of advertising, Seth puts across this big idea: *'Great marketers don't use consumers to solve their company's problem; they use marketing to solve other people's problems. They don't just make noise; they make the world better.'* You can see how it relates to leaders who want to make their marketing resonate in a changing world.

So, what is a hook? The hook is the line that hits you in the face with truth, something you rarely hear. The Psychology of Money was a big hit. The message was: 'The biggest value of money isn't to buy luxury goods but to gain control over your time and life – the ultimate form of freedom'.

The relatable story is a feeling that this author 'gets me'. For instance, *Bounce Forward* gave the message of resilience and, whether disabled or otherwise, using what's still open to you – and that's your attitude. Brené Brown is great at this; she's vulnerable in her stories and also offers research to back up why we need to be vulnerable too.

Attracting Clients

Many following the Viral Message strategy are author-publishers aiming for more client attraction. If you are primarily servicing others nationally, you might prefer private website publishing and set the cost of your eBook at $5 to $10 for people who want to get to know your methods better. As you would have a webstore or GumRoad account, you can then also get their email address, which is a huge advantage for the future.

Regular PDFs can be released too early and to the wrong people, so it pays to think about security. To make the eBook more secure against copying, you could offer an ePub rather than a PDF, although it's usually wise to ask your customers what they want or can access. I've had people say they couldn't open an ePub even though it was fine on iBooks app. Some would have trouble utilising Adobe Digital Editions eBook reader, or primarily they use the Kindle app and don't understand the difference. (Kindle does not allow transfer of files). That's why the PDF is ubiquitous. You can always set a PDF up to be more secure, using security tools inside Adobe Acrobat Pro or at least by using the Watermark feature inside Word.

Don't overlook the fact that quality book attributes and good niche audience research makes a big difference in word-of-mouth sales. Do your niche research with SparkToro and find what #, keywords and podcasts people look for.

Sell More with a Great Blurb

The equivalent of your shop-front window, the book description (blurb) is crucial to the final step of conversion to a sale. Remembering of course that the viral message is seeded: it has gone well at various media outlets, is known from speaking at Summits and/or retreats, and is all over your YouTube channel.

While it's hard to find an exacting formula, it's useful to examine what marketers have achieved with their own book blurb. Let's look at the blurb of Category Pirates' *'The 22 Laws of Category Design'* (2023) and break down how they did it.

Blurb Example

A.

This book is for a very small percentage of business people.

You see, most people in business are not trying to use Category Design to create a new category that changes the future and generates exponential new value. Instead, many people in business are trying to 'not get fired.' Many people want to go to work, make a contribution, and go home.

But Category Design is purpose-built for people who want to make an experiential difference, not an incremental better.

B.

Category Design is a business discipline that helps companies earn the majority of the value created in a specific new or different category of products or services. (Primary research on Category Design in Play Bigger, the first Category Design book, shows that in technology categories, one company earns 76 percent of the total market cap value created.) The 22 Laws Of Category Design is specifically tailored for entrepreneurs, marketing professionals, business leaders, solopreneurs, and consultants who 'think different.'

C.

It challenges conventional business and marketing wisdom, teaching you how to leverage the power of Category Design to create new markets, dominate existing ones, and build lasting companies.

In this book, you will learn:

- 22 Category Design principles that, when combined together, can help you become a Category King or Queen and make it impossible for someone else to 'do what you do'

- How to create new categories and redefine existing ones using a unique POV, Languaging, and a powerful marketing strategy called a Lightning Strike

- Detailed, real-life case studies on companies that designed and dominated new categories—from Apple's redefinition of the mobile phone category to Lululemon's reign over athleisure, Liquid Death's rise above bottled water brands, and more

- How to immediately begin applying what you learn, and work towards the outcomes you want, with 11 in-book exercises that help you engage your thinking, defy conventional business strategies, and drive company growth

- Why marketing your brand, instead of your category, is a faulty and selfish strategy, and how companies like Southwest Airlines, Bombas, and 5-Hour Energy win by putting Superconsumers first

- Lessons and quotes to help you continually reflect on Category Design so you can transform your thinking, actions, and outcomes forever, instead of for a few months

D.

You will be able to start applying these principles through 11 in-book exercises:

- Start Rejecting the Premise
- How to Find Your Superconsumers
- Put Your Category First, and Your Brand Second
- How to Frame, Name, and Claim a Category
- Be Different, Not Better
- Create Net-New Demand for Your Category and Company
- Build Your DAM the Demand Strategy
- Create Your Digital Air Offerings
- Figure Out Your Pricing
- Innovate Your Business Model
- Find Your WOM Super-Geos

E.

The 22 Laws Of Category Design is specifically tailored for entrepreneurs, marketing professionals, business leaders, solopreneurs, and consultants who 'think different.'

Through powerful insights, unconventional wisdom, and practical advice, this book will give you a unique roadmap to defy conventional thinking and create categories of consequence.

~

The first section, A, is calling out to alert readers who identify with the group of people who care about their vocation and want quantifiable change.

Section B explains Category Design, as it is particular to their ideas, and drills down on job titles of target readers. The part in brackets is supposed to push home that category leaders have more sway, but I think the way it is phrased is too complex.

In section C, the focus switches to what you will learn – starting with a big overall dream goal. (As Guy Kawasaki puts it: 'Sell the dream'). The learning outcomes bullet list is crucial, so they start with their strongest two. Number four is too wordy and weak, but number five contains the example and reasoning that would perk up many ears. This learning list must intrigue readers but not befuddle them.

Section D simplifies the learning in the exercises – which helps those who are into 'doing'. However, eleven points is not necessary and they take acronyms a little far. What is WOM? What are Super-Geos? DAM? I suggest keep this list to six things that solidify learning.

Section E repeats an earlier sentence (an error or purposeful?) to push the 'think different' message. The final sentence is their chance to crush it with a 'you-focused' life outcome.

~

As most of their buyers would be Substack readers of their newsletter, the Pirates did not need to frame their experience very much. But for you/your authors, it would be wise to add a line about a heartfelt mission. For example, 'Author Jennifer Lancaster is fixated on learning every area involved in self-publishing, not only to help her process but so that other authors can have it easier.' Therefore, the mission is not about what you do as a professional but what you are focussed on doing for your audience.

Remember to use Kindlepreneur's book description generator to get the 'bold' or larger font to show and try to use your industry's known keywords. Always get your book blurb proofread. Kindlepreneur also has a KDP sales calculator, for spying on what other books are selling. (*https://kindlepreneur.com/amazon-kdp-sales-rank-calculator/*)

12

Sales Funnels - the Hidden Secrets of the Online Gurus

A website is one thing, a sales funnel system quite another. As opposed to just book launching, some SAAS platforms benefit your micro publisher business in toto, especially if you're selling services or if you have a course for a particular niche.

To deliver eBooks and upsells at the early revenue stage, I'd recommend either of these:

Systeme.io is a budget-friendly sales funnel platform that includes features for landing page creation, email marketing, online courses, and it's simple. It is ideal if you are starting from zero.

Kit is a platform for beginner book marketers looking for a straightforward, no-frills marketing system. I use the Newsletter plan on Kit (free) and you can integrate paid products, but it's not designed for upsells. With this plan, you can run one visual automation (e.g. a welcome email series) and pick from many templates for the subscriber opt-in form, the code for which gets put on your website or blog. (Kit.com).

The email newsletter creator relies on using + in the edit window to add features and does not work well if using templates with too much text. The template should contain only text and parts you want repeated. My tip is to use a Starting

Point template, which is more flexible in the editor screen and provided me no trouble. You adapt it to your colours and can insert your own header and author signature.

Kit's Creator Profile feature is useful for those author-publishers who want to promote back to a multi-link landing page, like LinkTree.

There is a growing creator community, and people may hop on your list if you use Creator Network recommendations. This is the main selling point of Kit. Once finding someone who would be perfect for your audience (not directly competing) basically, you recommend each other. To get more out of this, you ideally reach out on social media to each creator in question so that they will recommend your newsletter.

Showing your recommended newsletter as a pre-ticked box on the second screen once someone subscribes to another newsletter, the viewer quickly decides whether they want those other newsletters – but they also might subscribe by mistake. Newsletter swaps at the author book funnel sites might be a better idea for connection.

It can be worth the fuss to get subscribers for nil extra work. First, you sign up, configure your creator profile, enable recommendations, then discover other creators to recommend by using the industry drop-down. See more about Kit at: *https://businessauthortools.com/plans* or *Kit.com*. Just like other EMS, you can use Kit in conjunction with a WordPress or SquareSpace website through API or plugin integration.

Why are Author Newsletters a Dream Tactic?

When building an information-based business, influencing new readers is all part of the process… and it's a long term thing. Monthly newsletters make this super simple. Rather than solely worrying over promos to offer your email list – you set up a systematic schedule of writing and emailing a newsletter. We build loyalty over time, which is not possible when algorithms change and people no longer see posts. In a fickle world, email marketing is your steadfast friend. Treat every subscriber like royalty and only send awesome stuff.

The beauty is, anything you put into a blog can be transferred to a newsletter, either with RSS setup or simply copying the details and headings. I would suggest putting as much real and actionable content into your newsletter as possible and don't rely on 'read more' links. My list showed that 1-3% clicked the 'read more' link, so I switched to one long article and the odd promotion of an ebook or course as a value-add.

An editorial piece at the top and personalised photo signature at the bottom is also a nice, friendly touch. Editorial introductions are for your own perspective, whether positive or mad with something in the industry. My reader preference is for witty, story based or column-style newsletters rather than ones littered with take-action-now promotional links.

Substack authors use that easy 'newsletter' platform to share their ideas, share their book chapter previews, and in some cases, to remind at launch time with a picture of their book. In fact, Malvin H Waller has used these and other methods to make bestseller on Amazon 29 times!

You could utilise Substack to gain a paid member readership once newsletter reader numbers hit about 100. There's little point in doing this too early. It is much better to get views on your book content previews and ideas.

Substack author Veronica Illorca-Smith has converted her many subscribers and past *Lemon Tree Mindset* book readers to gain a traditional publishing contract with a big Five. Her newsletter Substack growth has been aided by her collaborations with those on the up-and-up, as well as her marketing and brand prowess.

'Free to Buy, Pay to Ship' Sales Funnel

'Six Figure Sales Recruiter' is an example of a book sales funnel where the book is 'free' (pay $9 for shipping) and comes with a free training. Hohman is obviously not focusing on KDP sales (just a two line blurb and US$9.99 price). The whole strategy revolves around selling the book to attract companies who are recruiting salespeople. It's sold at the website and the upsell training is US$47. However, marketplace wise, the title is unfortunately confusing those who are sales recruitment consultants – a different market segment. Hohman's book website page at least has a simple call to action.

Brendon Burchard also did this method globally with his hardback 'High Performance Habits'. Shipping was reasonable considering the distance world-wide, however entrepreneurs here cannot cover shipping and printing with a 'free offer with shipping', due to increasing Australia Post charges. Unless it fits Large Letter, the actual cost of print & ship makes the offer absurd. (Free book, but with $20 shipping?)

Another problem arises when using your account's IngramSpark order form to send individual orders. Say your 144-page, 8.5 x 5.5" book is $8 to print, there is $2.20 handling, $10-13 to freight, GST, and at minimum this adds up to $21.50 already, with profits not considered. That's why authors arrange bulk print orders and celebs get the niche book printers to ship their books on order.

A very similar strategy is the $5 book offer on an expert's website, fed by an ad, which leads the consumer to the upsell funnel. The master at this was Paul Peace of Peaceful Profits. The upsell offer is usually discounted training that is offered either at point of sale or just after the $5 purchase. Another way to do the upsell is to host a video or instant webinar, with a 'book a call' button (selling high-level services).

13

Publishing Tools - for Micros & Author Agents

When you are getting busier with publishing, projects (with timelines), royalties management, metadata and so on gets more intense. For a publishing service business, we'll look at the following tools to keep everything moving along and growing. (Explanation may be in the next section to avoid duplication):

- Vellum or Atticus (for eBook formatting/production)
- PublishDrive (for digital/POD distribution and audiobooks)
- Ways to sell books direct, e.g. Woocommerce or PayHip
- Asana (project management) – see next section
- Spotify for Authors
- Kobo Writing Life or Draft2Digital

PublishDrive

PublishDrive is going to be a big time-saver for growing micro publishers who want to publish 'wide' (not solely on Amazon KDP). It is a paid-for SAAS.

Catering to self-published authors and publishers, this software platform helps you publish and distribute print books, ebooks, and audiobooks worldwide. They facilitate the files going to 55 channels and 400 stores and 240,000 libraries. So, you wouldn't need to use Draft2Digital, Apple Books, ACX (though you do need the narration done), Smashwords! Remember, both D2D and

Smashwords take an extra 10% over and above the usual shared revenue with the platform. IngramSpark takes 30 to 40% of ebook sales.

Whereas BookBaby is for newbies, PublishDrive is a portal to all the retailers at once. You would need the Docx or Open Doc, ePub file and titles, whether published or not, and the software guides you with the rest. If you want an audiobook on Spotify, sell print on demand to India or China, this aggregator will help you go really wide without taking a commission. They get paid by subscriptions.

As a lot of newbies tend to under-do their metadata, PublishDrive's AI assistant will really help create the best description, BISAC, KDP categories, price, etc. Here are **PublishDrive's** ongoing prices, in USD:

1 book	FREE
3 books plan	$13.99 per month
6 books plan	$20.99 per month
18 Books plan	$41.99 per month

Calculate whether you would be better off financially here: *https://calculator. publishdrive.com/* (Also remember the time-saving and optimisation features, and on the larger plans, the ability to capitalise on platform sales promotions).

The list of stores, including royalties and languages are here: *https://publishdrive.com/stores.html*

If you hate calculating royalties on spreadsheets, they have an add-on called Abacus, which is US$2.99 per title per month, and this ensures the right royalties are calculated for your authors. This would be helpful when there are currency conversions to also consider. I know I had trouble working out royalties from several places, going to several people, with a currency conversion and PayPal fee.

You will notice that on the list it's 10% wrong on Amazon Print. The usual royalty for internal sales at Amazon Print is 60%; Ingram is 45% usually (after print costs), though you can change this to suit sales targets. Audible's royalty rate for publishers depends on whether the title is distributed exclusively or non-exclusively:

Exclusive distribution to Audible: Publishers receive a 50% royalty rate

Non-exclusive distribution to Audible: Publishers receive a 30% royalty rate

While Google Play Books will give 50% on eBooks sold, if the publisher accepts the terms, they will receive 70% of revenue in Australia, Canada, or the United States. The exception is on titles that Google Play discounts randomly, which reverts to 52% royalty. PublishDrive tries to keep to the same listed pricing that the publisher wants. They say this avoids the automated price-matching by Amazon.

Audiobooks with PublishDrive

Once you are a multiple title seller, this will interest you. You can publish to Audible, Apple Digital narration and Spotify all at once if you have your cover and Mp3 files ready. What a time saver! Spotify acquired Findaway in 2021, so they have the titles, technology and distribution of that global leader.

Your chapter narrations must be in separate files and of good sound quality. They say that Audible and Findaway don't accept AI narrations, humans only. See how here: *https://help.publishdrive.com/how-to-upload-an-audiobook.*

Spotify for Authors

The new Spotify for Authors platform allows writers and publishers to track insights and analytics about their audiobooks' consumption on Spotify and to access a set of promotional tools. Spotify are working on new listening experiences, like having supporting material (images) from books time-synchronised to the story being read. That will be a game-changer.

As most indie authors are locked out now, what you'll do to prepare is go to *https://www.findawayvoices.com* and click the Register Free button. That way, when the ability to load onto Spotify goes live, you will then be all ready to do so. Upload instructions: *https://support.spotify.com/us/findawayvoices/article/how-do-i-upload-audio-files/*

The listener plans depend on the country. US audiobook listeners can subscribe to a $10 a month plan, while Premium users in countries like Australia, US, UK, Canada, Ireland and New Zealand can receive 15 hours free audiobook listening time per account (with optional upgrade).

Ways to Sell Books Directly

We've covered the reasons for selling books directly, particularly using your bulk stash bought at lesser cost in shipping overall. Now we'll talk about the online selling tools.

Having had an author website for years, it's reality biting that hundreds of books are not being ordered! However, if it's your plan to make pages worthwhile, visually stimulating (with High Resolution cover/other images), with simple buy buttons, then go ahead and install a plugin or PayPal button. If you set up email and postcard promotions, you might be able to encourage direct sales. (Relying on organic traffic does not work at the starting out level).

Plugins like WooCommerce are complex: you configure the system, set up books as 'products' with their data, set shipping rates, then connect to Stripe and PayPal (or WooPayments).

To set up a simpler e-commerce store with a payment gateway, you might choose a self-hosted platform like Shopify, select a payment gateway like PayPal or Stripe, and integrate them to process online payments. However, in both cases someone still needs to enter the book details, cover image, price, publisher, date released, and a few good reader testimonials. Yes, there is no getting around it – whether bookstore or book page – it's all work. (Also see PayHip in the next chapter for simpler still).

You need a Universal link to create traffic to the right Amazon marketplace or bookstore for them, and that's what several online tools offer. GeniusLink is great, because you can add in other stores too and get data on all the traffic. The plans are from US$6 per month (*Geniuslink.com*)

For digital indies going wide, **Books2Read.com** is the link page to set up, free of charge. Accessed from Draft2Digital.com or directly, readers can choose from Amazon, Apple, Barnes & Noble, Kobo, Google Play. D2D advise on how to use it.

∿

Case Study of a Successful Indie Publisher

Peter Holmquist has achieved significant success as a publisher on Amazon's Kindle Direct Publishing (KDP) platform over 10 years. One early success is a 27-page book on Anxiety he authored, which is now a free eBook. He moved on to get books written rather than write them himself.

Holmquist's success is really about his driven strategy. Key factors contributing to his accomplishments include:

Extensive Experience and Output: With nine years in the publishing industry, Holmquist has published more than 1,500 books on Amazon KDP, demonstrating his commitment and productivity. (Source: https://drivenpublishers.com/our-story)

Educational Content and Community Engagement: Through his YouTube channel, 'Driven Publishers', Holmquist shares insights, strategies, and lessons from his journey, giving guidance to a community of aspiring publishers.

Focus on Continuous Improvement: Holmquist emphasises the importance of adapting to industry changes and refining publishing strategies, as evidenced by his content discussing realizations and adjustments for upcoming years.

Sharing Success Strategies: He openly shares his experiences in building a seven-figure self-publishing business, offering practical advice and 'gold nuggets' to help others succeed in the field. He runs a Skool called 'Driven Publishers' and there he sells a training course for those experienced publishers levelling up.

∿

The amazement you feel when you find someone who made $4 million from publishing is akin to when you see the winner of the last lottery you entered. The odds in publishing calculated roughly by Derek Murphy: only 0.0025% of titles successfully sell $1000 and are in the top 10,000 rank at Amazon; even fewer percent once considering authors put out multiple books (blog at CreativIndie.com, 2018). Remember, that number is not even profit, and over half of book titles slip from the top 10,000 after three months.

Do you have the guts, determination and research focus to be in the 'success' crowd?

Kobo Writing Life or Draft2Digital?

Kobo Writing Life (KWL) is a free self-publishing platform that empowers authors and publishers to easily create, edit, and upload eBooks. By choosing to distribute your book through KWL, you gain access to a global audience, with millions of readers across more than 200 countries. Kobo partners with some of the world's most renowned bookstores. Kobo specialises in eBooks and audiobooks and has its own reading app (and e-reader range).

By publishing your eBooks or audiobooks directly to Kobo through KWL, you can access the books via an author dashboard and make quick changes and updates directly. You can choose whether you want to opt into the Kobo Plus subscription program (and which territories you want to opt into) and decide if you want to distribute to libraries. Kobo offers opportunities for direct authors for discount promotions, controlled via the KWL dashboard.

KWL offer 70% royalty on all Kobo titles sold and 50% on all Overdrive library ebook sales, with the big advantage of being able to set a library price (higher price). There is also an in-depth Help centre.

If you'd like to try KWL, you can also keep Draft2Digital. To use both Draft2Digital and Kobo Writing Life, just turn off the Kobo and Overdrive distribution in your D2D upload process, as you will be enabling it over at KWL.

Draft2Digital undoubtedly distributes to more eBook retailers than anywhere

– a big selling point – but remember, they take a cut from earnings. In most cases, it's 10% of the retail price. Most stores also take 30%, which leaves you with about 60% of the list price, less sales tax… (if you have authors, then you split this 50/50). The plus side: You can set ebooks at free.

In KDP Expanded Distribution, Amazon takes a 30% commission for books priced between $2.99 and $9.99 (you get 70%, less GST or VAT), and 65% commission for books priced below $2.99 and above $9.99 (a 35% royalty for you). With both KWL and KDP beating them in the fair price bracket, Draft-2Digital is now not looking so good in the royalty comparison stakes.

Just like KDP, Draft2Digital also offer special price promotions (controlled by you), which don't sell anything without the publisher doing promotional work. On experiments, I found these listed eBooks don't sell on discounts, and my theory is that unless people know the true value of your work, they won't buy at any price.

14

Publishing Tools for Self-Published Authors

(Including IngramSpark Royalties)

In this chapter, the intrepid self-publisher will benefit from these tools for repeated rounds of publishing:

- Reedsy Editor
- Atticus – to edit and prepare eBooks (and PDFs for print)
- ACX Tools – for Audible reach
- Google Play Books – for preparation and alternative audio/eBook platform
- Asana – for launch preparation
- Payhip – to sell books directly, simply

Reedsy Studio

Reedsy Studio is an online writing and formatting tool designed for publishing books with a clean, professional layout. Drafting is easy, with built-in collaboration features to enable sharing with editors and proofreaders.

For those publishing simple layout-style books, Reedsy Editor provides automatic formatting for print and eBooks, ensuring consistent typography, proper spacing, and ability to insert images without requiring advanced design skills.

You can reorder scenes or chapters easily, if written separately. The copyright and title page is automatically created.

It is easier to use than **Kindle Create**, and unlike Create, you can design eBooks that publish anywhere. There is a niggle, though. While it supports seamless export to EPUB and PDF formats, great for platforms like Amazon KDP and IngramSpark, in practice my exported print PDF made the table of contents (which is automated) a little off alignment.

Ultimately, Reedsy Studio is a viable free answer to book production for authors focused on the content itself. (*https://editor.reedsy.com*)

Vellum vs Atticus

Vellum is a book creation tool for Mac that allows you to edit and professionally prepare your book for publication. This software is free to download and use, but you'll need to purchase a package to export your files to publish. (Expensive for single use, US$249 for eBook and print).

Single users would be best to use an eBook converter service such as ISBN Formatting, IngramSpark (under Resources/Tools), or a known freelancer.

Mr Dave Chesson at Kindlepreneur thought he could do it better and came up with Atticus, which is for writing, editing and eBook or paperback creation (PC or Mac) and they both offer templates which can automatically do some of the work. If you have tables and images, they might need a little checking that it went through okay. It may not be totally controllable. (US$147 for unlimited books and ebooks, including updates).

See a review on Atticus: *https://blog.lulu.com/atticus-review/*. As the reviewer notes, Google Docs doesn't always play nicely with Grammarly, and in my case, with tables for some reason.

'It's critical that I create processes that are not only repeatable, but easy to follow. Now when I need to format an ebook or print book (in Vellum), I have instructions that walk me through all the steps.'
– nonfiction and fiction author, Ron Vitale, see Ronvitale.com/Vellum

eBook Conversion Types

Standard EPUB – a single and continuous flow of text and images that can be read on all dedicated e-readers and ereading apps. This is appropriate for most long form content and, with the proliferation of portable devices, it has the widest distribution. You can make an ePub from InDesign but it's not pretty. That's where you can use Calibre to fix small things up.

Fixed Page Layout EPUB – by design the page reflects the look of the original print book. This format is great for children's books, full layout cookbooks, and for any book where the integrity of the design of the print version must be maintained. This format has limited distribution. It is harder for the user to control the type size.

IngramSpark offer eBook conversions at US60 cents per page (based on your uploaded print file). Whenever I consider the difficulties of nonfiction ebook conversion I've encountered, I know it makes sense to pay a fee for an optimised and guaranteed e-reader compatible service. For simple books, there is Reedsy Studio or Fiverr ePub services for low budgets. Just ensure your ePub has a navigable table of contents (that one down the left side on a digital reader).

Asana – an App to Manage Launches

Say you are producing and launching a book in a three month window. You have a Book VA for uploading and review securing, a copy editor and a Cover Designer. You will do the marketing. Are you really going to use a spreadsheet? No! There are many fabulously useful 'project management' tools available, and each to their own, but I love *Asana.com*.

In 2019, I made a Book Launch plan out of their project template. It has three sections, which I changed to suit. Having a place for reviewing results is ultimately a good prompt as it helps you think about what worked—and what didn't. Some of the tasks I pasted were from a random book launch list found online. I was amazed when this app made each line into an item. Then I had to assign tasks (to the person responsible) and deadlines to each task. I also noted any costs. The tool reminds you via email of the associated deadlines.

Audiobooks with ACX Tools

Have you got the eBook done? Now, have you narrated each chapter clearly, with a microphone? Edited for jumbles and low noise with an audio editor (e.g. Descript)? Separated into chapters? Yes? Then you can use ACX to test your audio narrations for each book. See *https://www.acx.com/mp/audiolab*. You can also choose a narrator there or provide files yourself.

An audio editor can be a service person or a tool such as Audacity (a free recording and editing app).

Google Play Books – free Narration

To aim for world domination of audiobooks, Google Play is offering Play-listed eBooks free auto-narration. I stumbled on this and was amazed – several competitors were offering this same thing from $19.90 per month (lowest) up to $49 per month. However, it didn't work for me! Perhaps I set it up wrong but I'm not sure. See: *https://play.google.com/books/publish/autonarrated/#scroll-at-narration*

You also go on to list this audiobook for sale on Google Play and are then not behoved to Audible for all your audiobook sales, however their reader market is not as thriving. There are more professional ways to get an audiobook, such as hiring a voiceover artist or going to a podcast studio to record your book.

Books.By

This is a newer e-store and Print on Demand service in Australia. The tool costs US$99 per year the first year. It is unestablished whether: a) this website pays out, b) whether an author can maintain enough traffic direct to their book page for sustenance, c) if the books sell without previews. You can do the same thing with PayHip but for a small commission on sales (around 4%).

PayHip

Having your own book delivery system, aka page builder PayHip, means freedom. However, you need to be adept at driving visitors to your PayHip page. I let them choose by having a few bookstore choices on my online bookstore (using Mooberry Books plugin) and this can deliver an order back to me to fulfill. (It doesn't fulfill the order unless it's an ebook). People are wary of weird sounding words and so, in my experience, no orders came from here (400 clicks, no orders).

Your cover on PayHip looks nice and you can upload a preview of the table of contents and first page. Via your book page, using PayHip to handle purchases and downloads, you can earn 95% of your royalties, which is higher than Amazon and other retailers. Perhaps if one had a thriving blog/vlog/podcast and you explained PayHip and that it helps you build loyalty, people might buy. (*PayHip.com*)

New IngramSpark Decisions

Ingram Lightning Source have cracked down on poor quality print books and books with potential copyright issues. People who used to do this have found their books banned and not distributable. These are the type of books they don't want to help distribute:

- Summaries, workbooks, abbreviations, insights, or similar types of content without permission from the original author.

- Books containing blank pages exceeding 10%, notepads, scratchpads, journals, or similar types of content.

- Books or content that mirror/mimic popular titles, including but not limited to similar covers, cover design, title, author names, or similar types of content.

- Books that are misleading or likely to cause confusion by the buyer, including but not limited to inaccurate descriptions and cover art.

- Books listed at prices not reflective of the book's market value.

- Books scanned from original versions where all or parts contain illegible content to the detriment of the buyer.

- Books created using artificial intelligence or automated processes.#

In KDP, you can use AI in some books, as long as you tick the box that AI was used. That means cover art as well.

The Direct Distribution Model: How does it work for the big boys?

Publishers (who are vetted) can opt to use Lightning Source's direct distribution service in addition to distribution through Ingram, Bertrams, or other distributors and wholesaler Channel Partners. This allows a customer the option of ordering directly from the publisher. Many retailers and libraries currently work directly with publishers.

Nice! It's good to know what they can do for large publishers with deep pockets that is not offered to small ones. Read more at *https://IngramContent. com/publishers.*

Making Smart Royalty Decisions – IngramSpark

When setting up your book on IngramSpark, remember that a generous royalty-share percentage can make your book attractive to bricks 'n mortar bookstores. If your goal is to see your book stocked in physical stores, you'll need to structure your pricing and discount in a way that makes it appealing to retailers.

1. Understanding How Royalties Work on IngramSpark

Your royalty (or profit) is calculated as:

   ✒ **Retail Price – Wholesale Discount – Print Cost = Your Earnings**

Unlike platforms like Amazon KDP, which primarily sells directly to consumers, IngramSpark offers print-on-demand and distribution through Ingram Content Group, which acts as an intermediary between publishers and bookstores. That means bookstores don't buy directly from IngramSpark, they buy through Ingram Content Group, which takes an additional (undisclosed) percentage before passing the wholesale price to retailers.

Also, you cannot invite consumer orders via IngramSpark like you can through Draft2Digital for ebooks (with their Books2Read portal). The only solution for indies on IngramSpark to reach local independent booksellers, BookShop.org, is not available outside the US. As discussed, it's expensive to ship one book to someone; it's $10.70 + $2.20 for posting and handling on that inside order, when you could just post it off yourself from your bulk print stash. Typically, for a light book you'd pay $5.50 'large letter' post plus $1.50 for the envelope.

IngramSpark print orders can be 'rushed' both in printing or shipping. The shipping rate is what makes the difference, and you want tracking.

I'm no dummy. I worked out that I can offer website customers a better deal on postage by using the large letter post. Normally I keep a box of each book in my office. There are mailing houses that can handle this for you, should your publishing house happen to have a big winner. No need to worry about the possibility of success – places like SOS Printing in Sydney offer to print, ship, label and act as a Printer on Demand once you have proofed a book.

If you set a retail price of $20 for your book and choose a 55% wholesale discount, the wholesale cost will be $9.00. This means retailers will pay $9.00 to purchase your book.

2. Setting the Right Wholesale Discount

The discount you choose determines whether bookstores will stock your book.

55% Discount (Standard for Bookstores)

This is the industry-standard discount that makes bookstores most likely to stock your book. However, it results in lower royalties for you because a large portion goes to distribution fees.

Ingram Content Group keeps part of this discount before passing the wholesale price to retailers, meaning bookstores typically get around 40% off the retail price, not the full 55%. (I long suspected this but the compilation of various data from the LLMs has confirmed it).

40% Discount (More Author-Friendly, Less Attractive to Bookstores)

Some bookstores may still order at this rate, but many prefer the standard 55%. Your royalty per sale is higher, but bookstore orders may be lower.

30% or Lower (Discouraged for Physical Retail Sales)

At this level, bookstores won't order your book because they wouldn't earn enough profit on it. This option works best for online sales or direct-to-consumer strategies.

3. Factoring in Returns

If you enable returnability, bookstores are more willing to take a chance on your book, but this comes with a financial risk:

If a bookstore returns your book and you're in a distributor agreement, you pay back the wholesale cost and may also have to cover shipping and handling fees.

If your book is marked as returnable and destroy, Ingram disposes of the returned copies instead of shipping them back to you (avoiding additional fees).

4. Finding the Right Balance

To maximise both bookstore appeal and your earnings, consider these strategies:

If bookstore sales are a priority: Set a 55% discount and enable returns (marked 'returnable and destroy'). This gives your book the best chance of being stocked in stores, although there is no guarantee.

If you mainly expect online sales: A 40% discount keeps more royalties in your pocket while still making your book available to retailers who may order on demand.

If you're focused on direct sales (your website, events, bulk orders): A 30% discount or lower maximises your profits but severely limits bookstore distribution. You would also be getting bulk print orders so that your personal book profits are maximal.

Before finalising your book's pricing and discount choices, run the numbers carefully using IngramSpark's royalty calculator to see how each option (including colour) affects your royalties. A balance between bookstore accessibility and profit is key to a successful publishing strategy.

IngramSpark's ready reckoner under Orders has multiple choices, so be sure to check the right currency and the right print country for an order quote. The postage types are standard or express, meaning in practicality much the same thing, and the print rush times are standard (5 days) or rush (1-2 days). If you live in a place where mail often gets lost, choose the most tracked option.

For Those Going through KDP Print

If you prefer to publish through KDP but also other platforms, use Standard Distribution. If you tick Expanded Distribution, those retailer partners prefer not to order through Amazon (their competitor) and it will likely be fulfilled by Ingram Content Group or another partner anyway.

For standard distribution (60% x list price) – print costs = royalty

e.g. for a $15 book, costing $4.85 to print (60% x $15) – $4.85 = $4.15.

Expanded Distribution sales are offered at a lower royalty rate of 40%. You can use both Print on Demands or make life simple and choose IngramSpark for all distribution, albeit at a dearer rate for shipping books.

Order an Author Copy (not a Proof Copy) if you don't want the cover watermark from KDP Print.

Pleasing Retailers & Suppliers

TitlePage is the Australian book industry's supply chain service. It's used daily by over 1,800 bookshop owners and booksellers, as well as suppliers and library users. That's why small (and large) publishers want to use it, but it's very expensive to access TitlePage without APA membership, and the minimum of Small Publisher is a level up from Micro Publisher membership. TitlePage is the industry's ordering platform used by bookstores, but indie authors don't distribute their books directly to retailers in this way. Instead, they usually use print-on-demand (POD) services.

Good news! For most small indie self-publishers in Australia, **Nielsen Title Editor** is likely sufficient to expand all titles' meta data and check on things like cover image, blurb paragraphing, BISAC categories, etc. Here's why:

Nielsen's Title Editor allows indie authors to list their books in Nielsen Book Database, making them visible to bookstores, libraries, and online retailers. This is the primary requirement for discoverability.

The Australian Publishers Association (APA) Small Publisher Membership costs $220 per year. While it provides access to TitlePage, this service is mainly beneficial for publishers who are actively working with bookstores. (*https://www.publishers.asn.au*)

Many Australian libraries and bookstores rely on Nielsen's database for book metadata, meaning that an indie author's book listed with IngramSpark or Title Editor is still findable without TitlePage.

When might TitlePage be useful?

- If you are actively pitching books to independent bookstores and need a standard trade ordering system.

- You have multiple titles selling and want to manage sales professionally.

- You plan to work closely with bookstores that rely on TitlePage for ordering.

For most small indie authors, Nielsen Title Editor is a better first step, saving $220 while still providing essential book discoverability. You can always upgrade later. See: *https://www.nielsentitleeditor.com/titleeditor*

In the UK, using Title Editor is a must, because they don't have a MyIdentifiers ISBN assignment page like we do. If you filled out your ISBN Assignment in full, that information should travel to Nielsen Book's Database.

Fascinating Consumer Trends

In Jungle Scout's recent Consumer Trends Report, Amazon was the most popular search destination for consumers (56%), above search engines (42%), Walmart (29%), YouTube (13%), and Facebook (10%).[8]

Roy Morgan Research says that 7.9 million Australians shop on Amazon at least once a year, up 16% (2024).[9]

Gain reviews:

https://www.bookloverbookreviews.com/booklover-hub-authors-seeking-reviewers
https://www.boomerangbooks.com.au/content/main/book-reviews.shtml?
https://readersfavorite.com/book-reviews.htm

15

Reviews

There are many tools to help authors manage advance reader copies (ARC) and reviews, and some are also tools for post-publication reviews on Amazon, Goodreads, etc. Be careful that you don't just sign up for a place where it reviews only on their own site and not where readers will see it.

There is a strict rule with Amazon reviews: don't pay the person for reviewing. You don't want to get your account banned. Never use AI to write reviews in general, when logged into your Amazon account. You need this account to stay in good stead.

Here are the ways to get book reviews.

- Naturally, from strangers. For 1 in 100 sales, you will get a review, hence the problem with this method. It's also slow.

- You can reimburse book bloggers who expressed interest if they buy (called a verified review) or by gifting those people a paperback once logged in. You'll need to follow up by direct message or email, as people forget.

- With a tool where readers get shown your book and know it's launching. (See below).

- With an ARC (Advance Reader Copy) street team. If you have an email list of readers, it's easy: just ask for a review in exchange for a PDF copy (with security). You could alternatively ask them to share about the book on their socials, including Tiktok. Most book-loving sharers will need the paperback copy.

How do I get reviews post publication?

By gifting books to people (writers/readers) in your network who like reading those books! That's so simple, as KDP supply cheap author copies – simply buy the author copy and send it – or gift an eBook. They must have spent $50 on their Amazon account. When they have redeemed the gift and read it, their subsequent review will be 'verified'. Ensure you send a later email to prompt this as well. I also reviewed a book offered via a Press Release, which is another unique way.

How can an Advance Reader (ARC) team help?

As people need social proof in order to buy a fresh book from a new author, there is a lot of credence to using an advance reader team. It's best to choose the way you like: you can ask writer group buddies to be part of your team (quid pro quo, but at different times), ask reader friends, or go online and use a tool.

Here are the tools which rely on community and (after trial) are paid (around US$10 per month or $10 setup fee):

- Book Funnel BookSprout – can bring a reader email list to save money.
- StoryOrigin – pre-launch ARCs and joint venture launch promotions
- BookBlaze
- BookSirens directory (*https://booksirens.com/book-reviewer-directory/*)

Writer Tools that allow Collabs:

Kit.com – Creator plan makes it easier to get recommendations (newsletter based, not book based) and grow your list - $29 per month (more recommends) or free.

Substack app – Set up a niche publication. Making friends, following other writers is easy – choose those who are writing books as well, re-stack their quote, and invite them to interview you. Free.

16

Writing Hacks to Save Time

While it is tempting to use a chatbot for all our writing, don't if you want to avoid writing that's shallow and bland. However, when producing researched books or textbooks, you could use a Google AI tool which lets you upload a complex research paper or chapter and distil the essentials. This is especially useful when the paper authors use academic and scientific lingo. With this summary, it allows for clearer understanding and then with that understanding, you will write in your normal style. Google Notebook LM can do this, as it will also keep sources as it gives insights and answers scientific or psychology questions. Some businesspeople use it to upload articles and make a FAQs list for their website.

Research Before You Write

Before you start writing any kind of non-fiction, it's essential to research your target audience. This helps you understand what they're looking for, their challenges, and the angles that will make your book relevant and valuable.

Here are some methods I recommend:

SparkToro.com – A powerful tool to analyse audience interests. (5 free searches).

Forums & Online Communities – Places where people discuss topics in your niche.

Interviews – Direct conversations with your audience to uncover their needs, or with clients if this is relevant. (This can be in person after giving a talk).

Google Scholar tip – If writing a scientific principles-based book, review what's been researched and use correct science examples, not pseudo-science floating about the Internet.

By gathering these insights first, you'll save time later and create a book that truly resonates with your readers. Take notes and identify the people's main concerns, the topics that they're interested in and potential angles for your book.

Organising Your Topics with Mind Mapping

Some writers get stuck on the choosing and structuring of ideas. A simple way to structure your book is by using Tony Buzan's mind mapping method. This technique helps you organise topics visually, making it easier to see connections between ideas. I use this method to outline my books' main topics and subtopics before I start writing.

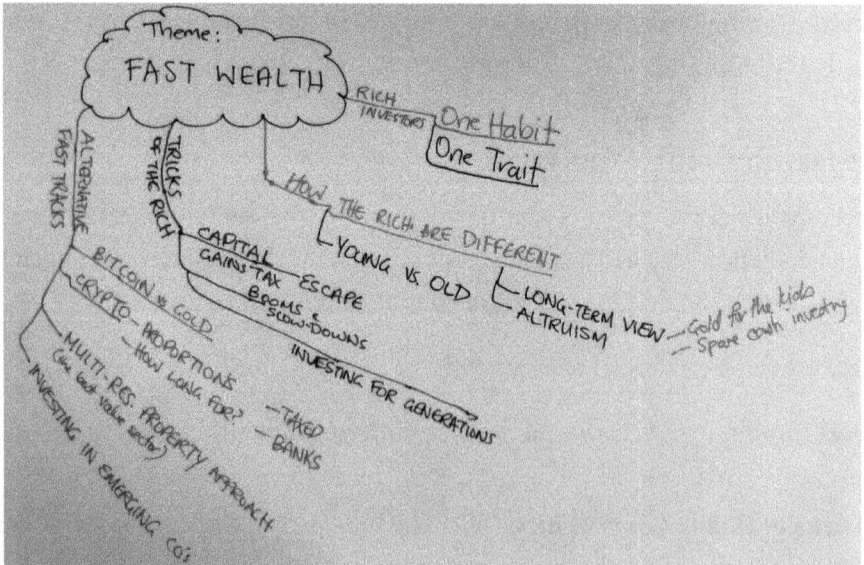

1 Mapping exercise on creating topics from a Podcast

Then, Mind Mapping™ is easiest due to the way our brain thinks radiantly rather than linearly. You use icons and coloured pens to make your mind map more memorable. The key is to write as few words as possible on each line. Just one word is often enough to associate other topics; other ideas will connect and just pop up. Trust your intuition.

After you've done this research above, start with that central topic and then have a play around like a preschooler. Get some A3 paper out and with colour pens, start mapping the central topic in the middle and then all the other sub-topics branching out from that. You just need a different piece of paper every time you start a new mind map.

The mind mapping also helps to sort out the top chapters deriving from the existing written content. We can't see past the clutter of a very long title, but it's easy once you pick out the keyword from the title. Each strand doesn't have to be a chapter name, just a niche topic at that point. Or perhaps you've identified a particular question asked a lot: a keyword from it can go on your mind map.

Journalists, you can match your brainstormed topics to articles that are in your article catalogue. Try to look through all the related articles on paper, as it's easier for your mind to identify patterns. If a Medium.com writer, you could copy over, then print the article names.

Sharpening the Saw

Stephen R Covey wrote about the habit of sharpening the saw because it's the difference between a man who busily cuts trees all day, getting nowhere, and one who spends time sharpening the saw – a metaphor for self-improvement and self-renewal (7 Habits of Highly Effective People). But what does this mean here?

It's about keeping those fears at bay by reflecting on your progress. Remember, you are neither 'a crap writer' nor 'an accomplished writer'… rather, you are always improving by learning techniques and practising thoughtful writing and editing.

The theory of non-judgement now permeates all I do, and I believe this helps writers feel that they're on a path of learning and creating, not static.

'Renewal is the principle – and the process – that empowers us to move on an upward spiral of growth and change, of continuous improvement.' – Dr. Stephen R. Covey

Identifying Themes in Your Writing

Remember to keep in mind the single thread that will be coming out amid your book. This thread keeps the work on track, and it is the answer to:

What purpose does your book have in the world and what question does it answer?

If you keep asking yourself this question throughout the revision phases, it will help you keep the work on point.

If you're writing creative non-fiction, you'll be reading the many books on it – but my opinion on what makes it interesting is the currency of the story. The scenes should be rich with present moment awareness. The main protagonist may be real and unknowable, but you, the author, get to make them human from the inside out. Your job is to do this work of imagining and to redraft until the reader can see it too.

Turning Your Blog into a Book

Many people have been blogging for years, but here's the reality: people are busy. Most of your readers only catch a fraction of your posts before moving on, meaning they may have missed some of your best content. That's why re-purposing blog posts into a book or eBook is a smart move. It allows readers who are genuinely interested in your topic to catch up in one place, without having to scroll through years of content. Even a curated collection on a theme can provide immense value when done well.

Of course, it's not as simple as just pasting blog posts together—there's an art to shaping the material into something cohesive and engaging. The key is to know your main insight, and know what pieces are the most important to educate and entertain on this topic. Say if you had 75 posts of a short (400-word) nature, that's 30,000 words, which is what I consider an ideal minimum bar for a nonfiction book.

Of course, if you're creating something meatier, you'd be aiming for 50,000 words. If you've got 100,000 words, you've gone too far. Theme and non-repetition is important. In each blog post there will usually be repetition of the past, and that needs to be culled.

If you write blogs, it's overwhelming to start with as you look through all the articles – but it gets easier. You're looking for a theme. Through all the topic hunting you're doing, you will think about the segment of readers: what they most want to know. Then look at your categories and your titles, or even longish social media posts: do you see a recurring theme? Look back through the year: what have you been talking about and what is that matches up with what people have most commented on or want to know?

Every blog is organised into categories and tags, along with the titles of each post. A good starting point is to go through your categories and post titles to identify the topics you're most passionate about. Look for common themes that could be woven together into a book. At the same time, align this with your market research—especially the problem-solution approach I talk about.

Side Note: If you're turning a blog into a book, your ability to group topics together depends on how well you've used tags and categories. In my experience, categories work better than tags for structuring content. A good rule of thumb is to have no more than nine categories on a blog—especially when covering a variety of topics. This makes it easier to find what interests you.

Post Analysis to Understand Popularity

If you want to take a more analytical approach, you can check your website data analytics to see which posts attract the most visitors. Look at where people are spending time on your site—what they pause on, click through, or return to. This can give you valuable insights into what truly interests your audience.

Sometimes, the results can be surprising. A few years ago, I wrote a post about the challenges of getting books into retailers and it gained hundreds of page views. It turned out that many independent authors were struggling with the process but existing resources didn't address their specific concerns. That unexpected interest highlighted a real need in the market.

Another useful tool is a word cloud, which highlights the most frequently used words and phrases in your blog.

Before I even knew *My Personal Brand* would become a book, I used mind mapping as an exercise. I noticed a pattern: many of my articles focused on personal branding from different angles, so I thought it would be the perfect illustration of mapping an outline. The theme was clearly personal brand, including positioning and identity.

Articles were all talking about a similar thing, though in a different aspect. It was enlightening to see that the message of 'building a strong personal brand prior to launching' was something I wanted to broadcast. Then I started writing the *Purpose Definition Statement*, which is my vision for why this book's theme and message is crucially important for those in my distinct audience.

Doing competitor and complementary book research is also important in order to find a gap. The easiest is to look at Amazon marketplace for similar topical books in the 'bestseller' column. Does your draft manuscript have the depth of coverage and tone of other books in your genre? It's not about being the same, obviously; you want yours to stand out. So, I always look for a little gap or niche market that I can angle it towards. For *My Personal Brand* I created a subtitle that included soloists and authors. I meant solo service providers, not singers. Again, get feedback. Because there are literally dozens of books on personal brand, and I wanted mine to be simple and accessible, 'My Personal Brand' it was.

Writing a chapter outline will now be a simple process because you've already done the hard work. Try to see the pattern between different subtopics and find out what's missing as well. The contents list (outline) will help, as you need to paste certain subtopics together so that it has a flow between the chapters and so that it has the same kind of style and message throughout.

Word, Google Docs or Atticus – it hardly matters what you use to type up the topics and article names. Some writers swear by Scrivener, which lets you reorder chapters and compile faster. Use whatever you prefer, as long as it's secure and easy to use.

Editing the Book

So, you've pumped out the first draft of your nonfiction or creative nonfiction book. Sweat, tears and research done. Now what?

Well, this where the real work begins. Lee Kofman calls this editing 'layering', as different edit rounds build up towards the final masterpiece. Within my book coaching program, I do the fun work of looking at structure and voice, and prompting the writer to fill in things that a reader won't know about. If they're telling a story and it ends suddenly, and I feel dissatisfied, I know the writer needs to add more detail and thoughts.

Lee also says, 'It is imperative to take off the blinkers... and turn searingly honest about the quality of our work'. [10]

If you cannot be a ruthless editor, then you need to hire one! It is only through years of writing, comparative reading, and copious re-drafting that a writer can become good enough to recommend. Not only this, but it becomes a pleasure to read such words – words that were considered and left standing after a thorough forest fell. Most novice writers are too close to their message or story, and that's what makes redrafting hard.

If you start writing in a completely different point of view or tone of voice, it can be a tough decision to scrap it all and match the tone or viewpoint in the first chapter/s, however, it is a necessary one. Readers can get a bit lost or annoyed if things jump around and, say, a creative writing section then turns into a journalistic style.

Tips for Re-reading and Redrafting

1. First wait a week or two and come to it fresh.

2. Read 3-4 chapters at a sitting, red pen in hand.

3. Print it out at Officeworks and give a copy to a critical person or someone who doesn't care about your feelings. Critiquing must be useful, not generalising all the writing in one comment.

4. Redraft after keeping connected to your work by redrawing a mind map or thinking/talking about the themes. This helps the unconscious come to the fore, and the unconscious self knows what to do.

If you've taken from your blog or writing platform, articles will still need a light edit, referencing and perhaps a quotable quote in the chapter starts. You'll ensure that it all progresses nicely along or at this stage you may need to hire an editor.

If you don't have the funds for an external editor, you can always try Hemingway or Pro Writing Aid or another editing app. Those will pick up basic kinds of mistakes, e.g. two words in a row, gaps before periods, or maybe passive voice in places, even when there is no possibility for anything but passive voice. Therefore, you need to guide it towards a clear and straightforward result.

It's good to think backwards and say: wait a minute, this person's just a beginner, they don't know what I'm talking about. What are we going to say in the introduction? Explain your point of view and a little background.

Final Steps in Preparing Your Book

Once you've organised your content, there are several important steps before publishing. These include writing your copyright page, a preface (if needed), acknowledgements (which are about people who helped in the book's creation), and references. You might also want to include bonus material and an about the author section.

A preface is not a foreword. While a foreword is written by someone you know who loves your new work, a preface is an author's note that explains the strands of reasons that brought this book to life and its 'big why' for the world. The big why, also known as the primary purpose, can be derived from our purpose definition statement (mentioned earlier).

Don't forget to rework the blurb to entice readers (see earlier section). You could use a formula to make sure it stands out in a crowded market, e.g. before/after 'the method', 5 life benefits, 7 Pillars, etc, for How-To or Self-Help. Or you could create intrigue in a narrative by describing the relatable situation and a life crisis. What happens to Helen? Will her dream come true or will it be foiled?

Bonus offers such as a specific worksheet, checklist, media list or calculator are the most sought-after things. Make your hyperlink to the offer short and pretty, with a shortener such as Bit.ly, or else make it simple, with 'www.publisher.com.au/bookbonus'. On that page, a recommended option is to use a subscriber form that also captures reader's emails for future newsletters and juicy offers from you. (*See* Newsletters).

Internal Formatting and Cover Design

The next step is formatting (called typesetting). I use Adobe InDesign, but there are plenty of other paid programs or free platforms available, especially for e-books. For instance, there is Reedsy Studio or IngramSpark Book Builder, which are free. (*https://www.ingramspark.com/design-a-book*).

If you want a polished, professional look for a printed book, this 'typesetting' step is essential. However, I recommend those who are putting out items like bulk romance books have simpler design software than people who are publishing how-to books with many subheads, diagrams and tables. The former could get away with using Microsoft Word if they know their page numbering/section starts. (You first insert sections before re-starting the numbering at 1).

Another key element is your book cover. A well-designed cover makes a huge difference. It helps your book stand out, and if clear and related to the theme, it increases sales. Hiring a professional book cover designer is a worthwhile investment. In Australia, a decent book cover designer charges from $350 per print cover (2-4 designs) and in USD, Red Raven Design charges $200, with three designs and three revisions, a 3D cover, a PNG & a PDF. See *https://www. designhill.com/member/redraven*. There are many designers on DesignHill.

Is it difficult for someone to learn InDesign from scratch?

Yes, it is. It's hard to learn and design as it is a quite a complicated program. But, it's a really good tool for print books: glyphs are right there; you can see what you're doing with spreads; you can see images are enough resolution and CMYK, and you can insert your photos just where you want them and have the text flow around it no trouble at all. (Glyphs are things like 'em dashes' and wavy lines called printer ornaments).

Affinity Publisher 2 is another publishing software that can be used. Because it is designed for publishing and production work, it lets you export properly to the right kind of PDF for Ingram (PDF-X1-2001/2003). It currently costs US$96 (AU$165) one-off for Publisher 2, rather than AU$29-$39 per month for ID (with InDesign's monthly plan, it's also expensive to cancel mid-year). Affinity also offer rival illustration and photo editing software, if you need those. (*https://affinity.serif.com/en-us/publisher/*)

If you want to try design software, always investigate what it can do because different software produces different printable outcomes.

With these kinds of page layout tools, the designer/you needs to have a handle on master pages, paragraph styles and character styles. This is so that you're not doing hours extra when you want to make a design change. Master pages are a concept where all type elements that repeat sit in a different area. For instance, page numbers are placed with 'Insert Special Characters: Page Number' on the toolbar rather than typing the number. (The InDesign window 'Pages' has Masters up the top). Other little things you need to know are where you put your right hand chapter-start pages and how far down your chapter starts go, which is easier with a 'facing pages' view and guides.

Mentioned prior, line spacing needs more visual breathing space, e.g. make height 4 pt. more than the font size used.

IngramSpark have an extensive guide: the Creator Guide, which your designer/ you must follow. They require a certain type of PDF and they require your black to be a 'rich black' and images to be at least 300 DPI. The minimum margin is 12 mm, but depending on the book size, 18 mm is more useful and 20 mm in the gutter, the bound edge. Their creator guide is available from IngramSpark. com under 'Resources/Tools' 'File Creation'. You'll also find the Cover Template Generator there, which is mighty handy for layout of the printed book wraparound cover, complete with barcode.

Distribution Options

Once your book is ready, the next step is distribution. While traditional distribution is a harder option, there are now many platforms for the self-published and agents of authors, as we have covered already. These platforms are called aggregators because they electronically distribute your book to multiple retailers, making it available to a wider audience. There is also BookVault, which I don't recommend due to quality variances.

Finding the Right Printer

One of the problems that a history or family biography self-publisher has is finding the right printer. Shepherding others with self-published books that are local history, family and children's books, it can be difficult to achieve perfect quality. Hardback is another choice.

As well as getting a sample from each known book printer, get at least two printing quotes for an intended trim size and length, just to be aware of what the going rates are for different sizes and paper types. When supplying a file to any printer, it must be in a Print Ready PDF file (high resolution) – not Word, so exporting from a proper publication program is required. They can normally help, with graphic typesetters who work at $80/hour+ to typeset and export your file properly. (This is a ballpark rate to make you aware that it's not a small bill).

Print on Demand is usually cheaper than buying in bulk from a printer (unless they are a Chinese factory), though you won't have as many paper or colour or embossing options and the quality is hard to keep consistent. Colour books that are premium, such as cookbooks, are going to cost plenty... I'm thinking of Blurb (Blurb.com) here, who specialises in printing of higher quality, rich colour books and magazines and are connected to Ingram for Print on Demand. One hobbyist said his photo-rich rock history books were costing $60 and he expected to sell them.

It all depends though: if you're preparing for a live event and you've got a certain number that coincides with the number of attendees coming, for example, 250 copies, then it's wiser to pay up-front for printing of a run and get the economies of scale. In this case, it makes sense to assess what great quality could be achieved at an experienced book printer. (See the Resources section).

Because of the risk involved in not selling large quantities, I advise novices to use print-on-demand and order in a box for use in review copies, library suppliers if your 'publisher' address is listed, personal sales, gifts to new clients, and a few for website sales. Unless you are already an influential type, order low numbers. For Aussies, I advise to use IngramSpark because they distribute everywhere and include library suppliers. The quality is also slightly better in colour covers.

Before you order at IngramSpark, you will see the individual and total prices, say $7.50 per book, then GST, postage and handling, and then you'll see the total at the end before you confirm the order. Note down how you can contact them before doing setup/orders, because things can go wrong – their email address is public; the phone number is not. IngramSpark have warranties on printing and boxing, however there are also matters in pre-press, like low resolution file errors, that you may need to contact them about. Prepare for a two day wait for issues via email.

It's so easy to order 20 more and wait 7-10 days that I am happy to run on a low stock. There is a great possibility of a revision being needed in my genres (marketing; personal finance) so I don't want 100 outdated books clogging up my office. Storing books is also a matter of keeping them dry. In the humidity here, covers out in the air immediately bend.

~

I hope this book has given you some food for thought on how to better run a Micro Publisher and assess your private or public publishing and marketing options. Your reader bonus is here:

Write a Memorable Book (short guide): *https://jenniferlancaster.com.au/ report-thank-you/*

Thanks for reading. If you enjoyed this book, please consider leaving an honest review on Amazon or wherever you found the book.

Endnotes

1   Alliance of Independent Authors, The Big Indie Data Drop 2024. https://www.allianceindependentauthors.org

2   Source: AnnaFeatherstone.com, Book Sales Statistics, Author & Publishing Industry Stats 2024 Running Tally.

3   William Blake story. Jacksons Art. https://www.jacksonsart.com/blog/2024/03/08/a-history-of-artists-books-and-how-to-make-your-own/

4   Automaated, 2024 Amazon Book Sales Statistics. Oct 24. https://automateed.com/amazon-book-sales-statistics/.

5   R. Fenton and A. Waltz. Amazon. *Million Dollar Book Formula.* https://www.amazon.com.au/Million-Dollar-Book-Formula-Forever/dp/194781494X

6   AustraliaReads.org.au; Australia Reads Survey results, 2023.

7   The Conversation, *Australians are Reading Less than Other Countries...* https://theconversation.com/australians-are-reading-less-than-other-countries-a-new-report-shows-why-243272

8   JungleScout.com *14 Staggering Amazon Statistics.* https://www.junglescout.com/resources/articles/amazon-statistics-2024/

9   Roy Morgan - Amazon press release. https://www.roymorgan.com/findings/9636-amazon-growth-in-australia-speeds-up-july-2024

10 Lee Kofman, *The Writer Laid Bare.* Ventura Press. 2022.

Little Black Book

Book Printers

Paradigm Print – Brisbane print brokers, who cost jobs for you and find the right printer.

InHouse Publishing – South Brisbane printers, experienced team.

Eureka Printing – Melbourne book printers, experts in full colour.

Cover Designers and Platforms

Red Raven Book Design; Print + eBook (Portugal) US$200 *https://www.designhill.com/member/redraven#*

GetCovers – Book Covers and Ad Images: from US$20-35 *https://getcovers.com/book-cover-design/*

NGirl Design (Gold Coast): from AU$330: *https://ngirldesign.com.au*

Typesetters/Internal Book Design

Working Type Studio: $2.40 per set page interiors. $360 + GST covers; *https://www.workingtype.com.au/recent-work*

Love of Books: $2.50 per novel page (up to 6 images); $2 per image edit; complex layouts must get quoted. *Loveofbooks.com.au*

Indexer/Editors

Gail, WordWright, Indexer – email: wordwright33@optusnet.com.au

Belinda Pollard –Accred. Editor: all types – *www.smallbluedog.com*

Jennifer Lancaster – editor/writing coach: nonfiction – enquiry@jenniferlancaster.com.au

www.iPed-editors.org – Directory of Editors, Australia

www.the-efa.org/membership-directory/ – Directory of Editors, US

Library Suppliers - Most are national

Let your local library acquisitions staff know that your book is listed with each:

PeterPal - see *https://www.peterpal.com.au/index.php/self-published-faq/*

ALS (S.A.) - *https://www.alslib.com/authors/*

James Bennett - *https://bennett.com.au/publisher-services*

Index

A

Advance reader copies 66, 111
Advance reader team 112
Amazon Ads 71, 79
Amazon Author Central 70
Amazon Author 'Follow' 71

B

Blurb 83, 121
Book blurb writing 83–84
Book description generator 63
BookFunnel 8, 65-66
Bulk orders 90, 105, 106

C

Category Research Tools 68
Chapter outline 119
Cover Template Generator 123

E

eBook security 83

H

Hooks 81, 82

I

InDesign, 101, 121-122

K

KDP sales calculator 86
KDP Select 70–71
Kindle Unlimited (Select) 76

M

Master pages 122
MediaNet Press Releases 58
Meta Ads 73

P

Purpose Definition Statement 118

S

Subscriber forms 87, 121
Substack writers 68, 89

U

Universal links 94